MODERN FRENCH SCULPTURE

MODERN FRENCH SCULPTURE

TEXT BY

GIUSEPPE MARCHIORI

HARRY N. ABRAMS, INC. · PUBLISHERS · NEW YORK

Translated from the Italian by John Ross

Library of Congress Catalog Card Number: 63 - 19570
All rights reserved. No part of the contents of this book
may be reproduced without the written permission of
Harry N. Abrams, Inc., New York
Reproduction rights reserved by S. P. A. D. E. M. Paris, Cosmopress, Geneva
Printed and bound by Stabilimento d'Arti Grafiche Amilcare Pizzi, Milan, Italy

Figure 1 - Auguste Rodin (1840-1917): *The Eternal Idol*, plaster, 1897.

WHEN DID SCULPTURE FIRST BECOME MODERN — AND WHAT DOES THE adjective "modern" mean, in any case? It would clearly be too arbitrary to choose a date — any date — as a precise point of departure, as a basis for contrasting one period with another. The opposition between traditional and modern takes form slowly, as the result of a slow development of aesthetic thought and the appearance of a few decisively revolutionary individual artists. The premises fundamental to change in traditional ideas about art are to be found in certain works which, even in the last century, anticipated the revolutions in taste that mark the twentieth century. Thus the family tree of "modern" can be traced as far back as one cares to go, according to how one interprets the adjective in terms of aesthetics and time.

The aim of this study is not to compile a history of movements and their underlying ideas, but rather to record the representative works and personalities that over the last half century have determined a complete transformation in the field of the visual arts. The study of these individual works and personalities will show the idea of "modernity" in all its varied senses, not as a vague, indistinct complex, but as

5

a continual development. In this way we may be able to give a reply to the original questions without attaching undue importance to a particular date or too precise a meaning to this treacherous adjective.

Our task is to outline the history of French sculpture from Rodin onward, or rather, from Rodin's mature work, with its outstanding clarity of intention and image, to the most recent works of sculptors who have come to look on Rodin as a classic, fit only for museums. So we see how relative the concept of modernity is, and that history is not a rigid framework, but a living reality in constant change. It may then seem less arbitrary to begin an essay on modern French sculpture with the Paris Salon of 1898, where Auguste Rodin (1840–1917) first showed the plaster of *Balzac*, which he had completed in 1897 after a series of studies and experiments begun in 1892. The long process of gestation of this statue is recalled by a succession of heads and torsos, now in the Musée Rodin, that is marked by cruel realism and dramatically intense expressivity. Rodin had set out to learn about his writer-subject with a scrupulous thoroughness that reflected his highly developed artistic conscience.

But in 1898 artists, critics, and public greeted *Balzac* with mockery and outraged indignation, thus perpetuating the tradition of scandal and public outcry that characterized the artistic life of France in the nineteenth century — from 1824, with *The Massacre of Chios* by Delacroix, to Courbet's *Funeral at Ornans* finished in 1849 and hung two years later, to Manet's *Olympia* (completed in 1863) in 1865, not to mention the clamor that met the first Impressionist shows.

Today, after all argument and polemic are exhausted, all passion spent, the monument to Balzac stands in one of the artistic centers of Paris, where Boulevard Raspail meets Boulevard Montparnasse, a stone's throw from the famous cafés: the statue now belongs to the everyday life of the city, a popular symbol of its intellectual history.

Rodin had come far from his *Man with Broken Nose* (1864) to the grandiose conceptions, in which the spirit of Michelangelo is never far off, of *The Gates of Hell* and *The Burghers of Calais*; these works drew him into a frenzy of work, into a tempest of argument and attack provoked by their excessive boldness in comparison with the monumental statuary of the time, and the masterpieces of Rude, Barye, and Carpeaux. In some typical works, *The Bronze Age* (1877), *Crouching Woman* (1882), *The Kiss* (1886), *Head of Pain* of 1892 (Plate I), and *The Eternal Idol* of 1897 (figure 1), Rodin had affirmed those traits of spontaneous naturalism and rich expressivity that were to appear under a very different light in the transfiguring synthesis of *Balzac* (Plate II). Rodin had studied the great works left by the Italian Renaissance, but he still remained attached to the tradition of Burgundian statuary with its search for a less idealized character. Balzac was not to become a hero, as the canonizing tenets of official statuary would have demanded. First and foremost Balzac was a man weighed down by the fatigue of his desperate daily work: he was essentially a writer, and did not lend himself to portrayal in top hat and frock coat. His fleshy, ravaged face was at once tragic and pathetic, and the obesity resulting from his sedentary life did not deserve the cruel realism of the *grassoni* modeled on Etruscan urns.

Rodin did not even concede Balzac the noble toga of neoclassical figures. He preferred to replace the hero with the man in all his painful reality: and so, in the course of studies aimed at showing a less external truth, a middle-class dressing gown

6

Figure 2 - Auguste Rodin: *Crouching Woman*, bronze, 1882.

was the vestment imposed on a nude figure seen through the artist's pitiless eye. Lamartine once wrote of Balzac, "His weight seemed to give him strength." Rodin remained faithful to this spirit.

Rodin's great invention is the dressing gown, modeled with sharp contrasts in its folds; the figure leans slightly backwards, completely enveloped in its drapery. Out of the mass of clothing emerges the hollow, powerful face, inspired and tortured with anguish. He makes a commanding figure, yet there is no rhetoric in the accurately observed movement with which he pulls the garment around his body, onto his shoulders.

Granted such ingenious insight, there could have been no other way of imagining a man of Balzac's stature, halfway between the real and the sublime, a superman, yet far from inhuman. And it was precisely this genius that put Rodin out of step with his times. His statue belonged to the future. When it was set up in 1939 at Carrefour Raspail, unveiled by such godfathers as Maillol and Despiau, the Balzac statue no longer seemed an archetype of modern sculpture. Nobody laughed then at the masterly statue, for over forty years had gone by since its first exhibition. And indeed, at the eve of the second World War, the first cycle of modern sculpture had just ended.

Rodin outlived his *Balzac*: from 1900 until his death his work was limited mainly to portraits and numerous variations on the theme of embracing nudes, from *Sin* in 1900 to *Nymphs* in 1910. His fame as a great sculptor in the tradition of Michelangelo had become so widespread that Rodin, in his house at Meudon, was an almost legendary figure, though evidently human in his weaknesses and moral compromises. The story of the decline of his physical and mental powers makes very painful reading.

But before the signs of decay began to show, this great renewer (along with Medardo Rosso) of nineteenth-century sculpture, in his nostalgia for the antique, or the *grande stile* of Michelangelo, had looked on the human body as the ideal measure, but without translating it into new aesthetic canons. Rodin's majestic sensuality flowed with a natural innocence into the entwined bodies to show the creative force of nature. Always pursuing his great dreams, Rodin was unaware that any other art existed in his time. "Art is dead," said the old man in 1911. "Humanity no longer knows what to do with artists. Men won't meditate, contemplate, or dream; all they want is physical pleasure." Rodin had a statue before him then, *The Thinker* (1880), an athlete forced to sit down and think; and in the name of thought, the positivist divinity of the middle-class nineteenth century, the sculptor set out to condemn a present from which he felt shut out because it no longer believed in a love of beauty. He, Rodin, had created *Balzac* and modeled the back of the *Walking Man* with an imagination free from all academic conventions and completely unconnected with the times. In Rodin's boldest works there is a sort of dynamic energy in the structure and surfaces that modern sculpture was later to make its own, though in terms of totally different formal conceptions.

While Rodin was denouncing the times, Matisse and Picasso had discovered African sculpture, and Cubist sculpture, heralded by Picasso's *Woman's Head* of 1909 (figure 5), was about to make its appearance. But before moving on to Cubism we must mention the work of Bourdelle, Maillol, and Despiau, who were closest to Rodin and carried out their work at the same time as the sculptors of the avant garde, but incomplete isolation from the aesthetic doctrines and experiments of those artists.

After studying under Falguière and Dalou (one of Rodin's fiercest adversaries), Antoine Bourdelle (1861–1929), the artisan from Montauban, born of a carpenter father, with one grandfather a weaver and an uncle a marble worker, had the good fortune to enter Rodin's studio as an apprentice. His master immediately made him feel the overwhelming dominance of his personality and the influence of Michelangelo, but Bourdelle did not accept all this passively. What saved him was what he had inherited from his craftsmanly ancestors: a tradition of *métier*, which had an important moral effect on his development as a sculptor, giving him the ability to face the most ambitious and demanding compositions as a good workman who knew no technical obstacles.

Dominated as he was by large-scale visions, Bourdelle was lucky enough to be given many opportunities to work in monumental proportions, from the *Monument to the Resistance of 1870–71* in Montauban to the equestrian statue of Alvear in Buenos Aires, from *Hercules Archer* to the high reliefs on the Théâtre des Champs Elysées, from the Mickiewicz monument to the low-relief frieze on the Marseilles theater: he showed the "passion for greatness" that Suarès, the French D'Annunzio, speaks of. During the most exciting years of the artistic adventures of Picasso, Matisse, Brancusi, Laurens, and Arp, Bourdelle interpreted art in his own way, with a highly imaginative idiom and a magniloquence of gesture. Suarès' masterly rhetoric forms a counterpoint: "Whatever one may think of him, Bourdelle is great because he has never lived for anything but greatness; he has always sought after greatness, conceived and done everything possible to render it present in a time when it was neglected, when it seemed dispensable. The fragment cannot be a complete work. One column is not enough. We must have the entire temple." Sound the trumpets, by all means, but the "temple" is often less valid than the column, or indeed the capital. Bourdelle had unconsciously created his own archetype of genius, as so often happens with talented autodidacts. "Life has been my school," he used to say, and life for him was a long succession of works — 880 sculptures and 6,000 drawings, temperas, watercolors, and oils — which one studies now, searching for the vitality of a fragment, the authentic quality of a detail. Thus it is useless to speak of Greece, or of medieval French sculpture, with a view to explaining the sources of the immense architectures of horses and heroes erected by Bourdelle. The imposing frameworks support the expansions of a theme that seems better defined and crystallized in the sketch modeled beforehand, following the original idea more closely. In this way small bronzes acquire more independent value and poetic significance, for example, the *Penelope* of 1908 (Plate IV), the portraits of Ingres and Daumier, the small heads of Hercules and Apollo, and some studies for *Beethoven*. There are many failures in the series of studies inspired by this ideal type of Romantic genius, with his turbulent hair falling over his broad brow and the emphatic features of a tragic mask. Bourdelle followed the traditional iconography, starting from a baroque interpretation of Beethoven's death mask. Like Rodin, Bourdelle wanted to make his own Balzac. And he succeeded in the fourth study, the large, expressive sculpture of Beethoven done in 1901 (figure 3), perhaps the most expressive sculpture of his entire career, which is pushed to the verge of a truculent caricature. Bourdelle let himself be guided by his talent for improvisation, by the animated élan of forms projected in space, but this baroque rush of movement was followed by the archaic immobility of hieratic figures, archetypes, and allegories drawn from a composite, culturally derived world. His imagination was always precariously poised between *le calcul et le rêve*, drawn into creating the Colossi of an absurd mythology. Yet only rarely in Bourdelle's art do we find a synthesis of opposites in the singularity of style or in the unity of a truly poetic image.

The craftsman made up for the shortcomings of the artist, who was often carried away by the desire to "do things on a large scale." The model set by Michelangelo's extraordinarily powerful imagination, which had touched off fertile, inspired reactions in Rodin, appeared to Bourdelle in a false perspective, artificially inflated by the "heroic" literature in which the sculptor had steeped himself. As a result, the synthesis took place only in the small-scale works, in those works of secondary importance which the artist must have considered unworthy of the huge monuments conceived for the greater glory of the cities of France and America.

Unlike Bourdelle and Rodin, Aristide Maillol (1861–1944) devoted the first forty years of his life to painting, leaning first toward Gauguin, then to the Nabis (Bonnard, Vuillard, Roussel) and Maurice Denis, showing a particular interest in applied decoration (rugs, tapestries, and ceramics) and wood engraving. His vocation as a sculptor appeared unexpectedly and at the beginning (1900–04) seemed inspired by a certain late Greek and Roman realism, because of its "Mediterranean" spirit rather than close cultural ties. In 1905 he was entrusted with the execution of a monument to Auguste Blanqui, which Maillol conceived in the form of a vigorous woman leaping forward but held back by the chains that shackle her wrists. This was *Action Enchained* (1906) in which the sculptor proposed the prototype of his shapely women, those country-bred Pomonas who breathe health and sensuality.

Maillol's art presupposes a humanist conception of time: a contemplative calm during which each image is allowed to mature, and is then translated into plaster or stone in a long process of elaboration, similar to that of antique masters.

When he began weaving fabrics and rugs, Maillol dyed his wools with colors extracted from mountain herbs and flowers, following rudimentary techniques: when he engraved the woodblocks for Vergil's *Georgics* and Ovid's *Ars Amandi*, he looked for a paper suitable for his classical subjects and, finding none on the market, made it himself with home-made equipment. Later, when he began to carve stone and model clay, Maillol devoted himself, like a humble craftsman, to perfecting the ancient techniques that can only be learned through work. He used to say of stone, "The harder the better," for he loved to attack it with hammer and chisel, reducing it into full, compact volumes, precisely because he aimed at "understanding" his material.

This summary information allows us to reconstruct the essential outlines of the timeless personality of this artist, always faithful to his concept of truth, with profound moral determination and touching innocence.

The first time he visited Greece, Maillol rediscovered the light of Banyuls-sur-mer, his own Mediterranean village, where he spent the winter months in perfect solitude. The two lands have a common civilization and share a sort of idealized geography: Maillol, then, belonged to Greece both by choice and by tradition. Indeed, he once said: "I look for architecture and volumes. Sculpture is architecture, balance between masses, tasteful composition. This architectural aspect is difficult to achieve. My aim is to rejoin Polyclitus. I always start from a simple geometrical figure, a square, a lozenge, or a triangle, because these are the figures that stand up best in space."

Thus we have the basic forms of Classical sculpture revived and adapted to the immediate reality of Maillol's vision. The female nude provides the module within which the artist sets out the elementary principles of his composition. The square, the lozenge, and the triangle are the hidden proportions contained in the harmonious structure of his nudes. But each plan is dominated by his feeling for nature, which breaks out in every form to render it actual, immediate, far beyond any slavish reference to the antique.

Mediterranean, Pomona, Leda, Venus, Flora, Night, and *Ile de France* (Plate V) are certainly the works that reflect most faithfully Maillol's ideas and his healthy, naturalistic inspiration. They all fit naturally into their geometrical frameworks, and the resulting solidity of their formal architecture is still alive with the vitality of the image, which is also the vitality of a mind that can never cut itself off from nature, that "sees" its figures in the light and air of a real countryside in which they then — and only then — become sculpture. Maillol's nudes are the concrete forms of a world in which reality and fancy seem to coexist in a harmonious synthesis, suggested not only by contemplation but also by a reappraisal of art which enabled the artist to discover some of the essential values of archaic sculpture.

His straightforward, "primitive" nature — that of an artist lost in the wrong century — affirmed itself all the more outside the bounds of the initial Alexandrine realism. Finally, he came to prefer the masters of Olympia to those of the Parthenon: he even said that Praxiteles' *Hermes* was "... pompous and stuffy ... carved out of kitchen soap." And he concluded: "Art is sensuality. How can we create it except through our senses? Besides, look at the nature outside this window ... Here it is impossible to make frigid art. Nature is good, healthy, strong. One has to see inside it and listen to its language." And he did listen to it, for old Maillol, too, was good, healthy, and strong — a pure in heart. *Summer, Venus with Necklace, Seated Nude, Three Nymphs* of 1936–38, and *The River* of 1939–42 (Plates VI–VII) clearly express the exact quality of this "listening," which was then transposed into a vision of calm formal purity. The ideal of *stasis* or that of movement inherited from archaic art gives a solemn gravity to his works, made to be set in a space filled with light. Maillol's nudes are not for museums; they were conceived in the sun-drenched woods and fields of the south, between reading the *Georgics* and contemplating a rural landscape.

But for Maillol pastoral life was no academic Arcady: it was a human situation, sincere, spontaneous, and necessary. It had much in common with Renoir's human situation in his hermitage at Cagnes, which was enlivened by the presence of his rosy nudes, those sturdy peasant models. Maillol was a fantastic character for his time, but his humane truthfulness could be disconcerting. "I invent nothing;" he said with the humility of the true poet, "it would be as foolish for the apple tree to claim it invents its apples."

His presence during the period of the boldest artistic experiments and adventures could have implied condemnation of the events that had led to the schism between modern and traditional sculpture. Instead, in a time opposed to durability, the existence of this artist, coming from a remote civilization, was somehow reassuring because of the halo of eternity that seemed to surround his works. When the octogenarian Maillol carved *The River* with the same youthful vigor and vehemence that had marked *Action Enchained* forty years before, many avant-garde movements in Europe had completed their historical span. These two works mark the limits of the entire cycle of Maillol's nature in its straightforward stylistic continuity, untouched by outside contemporary happenings. There can be no comparison between the two phenomena, though they are brought close in time by reasons of historical and poetic coincidence.

Charles Despiau (1874–1946) had contacts with Rodin and Bourdelle and stylistic affinities with Maillol. His female nudes, which can be compared with those of the master of Banyuls for their structure and the quality of their modeling, are nevertheless distinguished by sensitive grace and a certain pained nobility of expression. Despiau owes his fame mainly to his portraits, the fruits of his attentive study of Italian Renaissance bronzes, which provided him with ideal models of style.

These portraits, from *Paulette* of 1907 (Plate IX) to *Princess Murat* of 1934, contain a certain inner vibrancy that enlivens the finely modeled and shaded faces and underlines their human and spiritual aspects on a plane of high formal dignity. Despiau is heir to the acute, witty portrait tradition of the French eighteenth century, and combines this with an austerity derived from fifteenth-century Italian models. He tackled statuary with just as strong a sense of commitment, but along very different lines from the "monumentality" of Maillol.

Eve of 1925 (Plate VIII) and *Standing Nude* of the same year are two typical specimens of Despiau's sculpture, whose careful elegance never falls into the mannerisms of a Malfray or a Gimond. His nudes are the sculptured equivalent of certain Bonnard nudes, with their incisive outlines and intimate light, without violent contrasts, which shows them off in the fullness of their first youth.

A new flux of avant-garde activity in the arts was beginning throughout the world when Despiau died, half-forgotten, in 1946. But he had exercised a dominant influence on sculpture in Europe, particularly in Germany and Switzerland, in the years between the two world wars. His calm, restrained work is distinguished by an *esprit de finesse* which, though inimitable, inspired hosts of imitators. Despiau's success is closely linked to the same forces in the current of modern sculpture that produced personalities like Rodin, Bourdelle, or Maillol at the precise moment when sculpture was undergoing transformations in its very substance, matter, and technical procedures, using a dynamic energy unknown to Cubism and the Constructivist and Neoplasticist movements, which were involved in creating a new formal purism.

In 1907 Despiau sculpted the portrait of *Paulette* and one year later Brancusi took a block of stone and hacked it into *The Kiss* (Plate XVI), a gravestone that exalts life and occupies a place in modern sculpture equal in importance to that occupied by Rodin's *Balzac*. But before we mention Brancusi, it is better to deal with the work of the painter-sculptors, Matisse in particular, because Picasso and the Cubist sculptors will have to be discussed at greater length in connection with avant-garde sculpture and the personalities, from Brancusi on, that represent it.

Sculpture by painters is one of the most vital innovations of the nineteenth century, especially in comparison with the work of the better-known "pure" sculp-

12

Figure 3 - Antoine Bourdelle (1861-1929): *Tragic Mask of Beethoven* (Study IV), bronze, 1901.

tors. Who can be set against the plastic genius of Daumier, with his masks of human stupidity, avarice, or unity? Who can rival the dynamic sense of Degas' dancers, suspended in mid-air in the most daring dance steps? Who can compare with the imaginative freedom of Gauguin, his discovery of primitive, barbaric, and popular arts? The three men embody three universal propositions suggested by the desire for concreteness expressed in the plastic image, whether in relation with painting or, as in the characteristic case of Daumier's *Ratapoil*, on the plane of complete formal autonomy. The sinewy, agile figure of *Ratapoil* and the looser movements of Degas' dancers prepare the way for the expressive deformations of Henri Matisse (1869–1954), so similar to those carried out in painting by the Fauves. Matisse's painting is rich in motifs and traits that are in continual opposition to the rigorous academic education that lay at the root of his artistic development. A continual struggle within himself, in search of complete spiritual liberty: this was the life of Matisse, from the early days in the atelier of Gustave Moreau (some of Moreau's works show him to-day as a precursor of abstract art) up to his extreme old age, when he used colored papers, cut and gummed, to "paint" the most pure and luminous decorative friezes of our times — the famous *papiers collés*.

Matisse began to sculpt in 1899 and continued until 1912, at which time he had executed 68 sculptures. His elegant graphic sense, which controls the most harmonious combinations of coloring in terms of spatial values, is to be found again in the wavy outlines of his sculptures, modeled with an almost baroque richness of broken, painterly planes. The exotic and archaic, filtered through the refined taste of a culture in the service of creation, suggest the models for these statuettes of female nudes, the three-dimensional proof of the vitality of certain forms, often limited to the pure linear profile. Against academic virtuosity Matisse sets the open-minded freedom of formal analysis. Through distortion and decomposition, the result of his analytical experiments, Matisse creates the expressive types of his standing or reclining figurines, in all the most mobile or relaxed positions of his painted odalisques. Sometimes one can detect the soft cadences of Art Nouveau in these figures, but even this stems from the immediate, intensely tactile pleasure of modeling the sketches.

Matisse's expressionist syntheses, transposed into the more generous dimensions of his high-relief nudes, take on monumental solemnity. Occasionally, as in *Tiéré*, one notes a curious stylistic affinity with the ironic, classically inspired masks of Picasso. Such exchanges were frequent between Picasso and Matisse, as was to be expected from the nature of their research and the cultural climate they shared.

The *Reclining Nude* of 1907 (Plates X–XI) belongs to the most interesting phase of Matisse's activity as a sculptor: it can be attributed to the Fauve period by the manner in which the dissonant boldness of coloring is translated into a vitality of plastic forms. Such a relationship is difficult to achieve, but it exists and serves all the better to explain those sculptures in the context of Matisse's poetics. In the end, the products of parallel, closely linked explorations can be mutually independent. The principles of analytical decomposition and distortion applied to sculpture assume, in the works of Matisse and Picasso, unforeseeable aspects, completely new, with endless possibilities for development. The same thing had happened with the works of Daumier, Degas, and Gauguin, begun in a spirit of experimental curiosity and

14

resolved in the domain of poetry. In this sense, Matisse's sculpture is by no means an activity marginal to painting: rather, it illuminates and completes his complex personality.

In his work on twentieth-century sculpture, Werner Hofmann considers the possibility of contact between Derain and Brancusi, since Derain's *Crouching Man,* enclosed in the clearly limited mass of a block of stone, can, in spite of important differences in style, be compared with Brancusi's *The Kiss,* which is also formed of a single stone block in which the figures are indicated with a minimum of relief. With Gris, who was closely linked to the aesthetics of Cubism, Derain is one of the few painter-sculptors of the historical period of the avant garde. (Renoir is a case apart and simply experimented in sculpture with the plastic exuberance of his abundantly built models.)

Georges Braque (1882–1963), all of whose artistic activity is dominated by an age-old passion for craftsmanship, introduced skillfully executed copies of wallpapers into his painted surfaces, as he had previously done with imitations of wood, marble, books, and newspaper headings. Then with Picasso he invented *collage,* sticking actual pieces of wallpaper, newspaper cuttings, corrugated cardboard, pieces of wood, scraps of cloth, and matchboxes on his canvas or board, often anticipating the *Merz* (collages and mixed-media compositions) of Schwitters which were freer and more inventive by comparison with the order and structural organization of Cubist composition. In Braque's work, as in Picasso's, there is a movement toward relief, a sort of tactile space in which real objects, transposed to the plane of art, acquire a new dimension and meaning.

The first real sculpture by Braque, after his experiments with mixed-material compositions closely linked to painting, is the *Standing Woman* of 1920. But immediately after, he returned to the direct relationship, in paintings and engravings, with the series of mythologically inspired plasters painted in black or other colors and engraved. The same is true of his polychrome low-relief ceramics.

In his retreat at Varengeville, where he spent the years of the second World War, Braque devoted himself almost exclusively to sculpture. He carved and polished the chalky stones he found on the beach, and modeled the *Horse's Head* of 1943 (Plate XIII) and the *Ibis* of 1945, interpretations of archaic themes, in the idiom of what Dubuffet calls "cultural forms." Modern civilization can be equated equally well with Braque's archaism as with the technical mechanism of Schöffer: that is, it can embrace the two poles represented by nostalgia for the antique, on the one side, and scientific prophecy of the future, on the other.

Braque is perhaps the most "French" of French artists, by virtue of his ability to synthesize rational calculation and the irrational of the poetic vocation. In his archaeological and primitive sculptures, such as *The Nile* of 1942 (Plate XII), he uses this "cultural" return to first sources to express his own feeling for nature, which even the most decadent stylistics cannot stifle.

The significance of certain natural forms, long and thoroughly studied by Braque in his precious sketchbooks, becomes defined in the symbols and allusive signs that represent these forms: they are the result of a process of abstraction carried out with the aim of discovering a more intimate formal truth.

In his various periods of sculpture, Picasso approaches nature with an intuitive, sensual brutality. He always resolves his personal or cultural reactions and memories in the act of creation: for him, culture becomes a pretext to be transformed in the truer, more vital reality of his inventive genius. Dubuffet's idiom of ironic metamorphosis is purely contingent, depending on the possibilities of the material used, whether wood, sponge, tin foil, or *papier mâché*. Dubuffet can take a root or a branch and give it meaning, rich in Surrealist undertones. The figures of *art brut* reappear, spellbound and anonymous, in the bizarre iconography of *graffiti*, interpreted by Dubuffet with a highly civilized humor.

For Fautrier, sculpture was a curiosity to be explored: his experiments in 1929 and 1945 gave only modest results. On the other hand, Ubac finds in sculpture a link with his native Ardennes, which is rich in slate, his favorite material. Using a technique of his own invention, he cuts and furrows the opaque surfaces of his polished stele-like slabs and reveals vegetable or animal figures in a sort of flattened relief governed by a dominantly graphic sensibility.

In the last few years, the links between painting and sculpture have become more frequent in the ambiguous forms of object-assemblies and mixed-media compositions pioneered, in very different historical contexts, by the Cubists, and by Schwitters, Arp, and Max Ernst.

Contemporary accounts on the work of Constantin Brancusi (1876–1957) agree on one point: the antique simplicity of the man, who spoke in aphorisms and possessed a miraculous gift for transforming even the humblest object into sculpture. Indeed, Brancusi had unshakable confidence in his manual ability as a craftsman-poet: this protected him from any academic or cultural influences. He refused to enter Rodin's studio and had no contact with Maillol; in fact, he was a completely "home-grown" genius and always remained fiercely independent even in the heart of a great city like Paris. In the solitude of his studio, now reconstructed in the Musée d'Art Moderne in Paris, Brancusi always made everything with his own hands, just as the peasants in his native Romania had done: not only everyday objects, like chairs, tables, and stools, but also the bases for his sculptures, generally in wood, which are essential complements to the sculptures themselves. Brancusi had drawn a veil between himself and the outside world, so that he was able to maintain an absolute purity of vision, in many ways comparable with a sort of mystic clairvoyance. Contemplation of his own work left him eternally dissatisfied before the endless task — which, for the sake of all-over perfection, he was never in a hurry to complete.

The memories of the few people who were close to him are supplemented by his own thoughts, which throw more light on his moral and spiritual world. He used to say that "theories are valueless samples" and "only action counts. . . . It isn't difficult to do things: the difficult part is getting into a fit state to do them."

It is not, then, simply a question of the will to act. To prepare himself for action, Brancusi paid the price of years and years of persistent work to reach a flawless form. This was his artistic moral code, his spiritual strength, and the conception of a form invariably corresponded to a perfect realization: one has only to think of the *Fish* in marble (1928–30) and in polished bronze (1927), *Little Bird* (1925), the polished bronze *Bird in Space* of 1940 (Plate XVIII), *Cock* (1941), or the

Figure 4 - Constantin Brancusi (1876-1957): *Adam and Eve*, wood, 1921

marble *Seal* of 1943 (Plate XIX). In 1908 he sculpted *The Kiss*, in 1912 the gilt-bronze *Maiastra* (Plate XVII), in 1913 one of the portraits of Mademoiselle Pogany, and in 1922 *Leda* — a series of works that shows the truthfulness of his "seeing far," as if, in his own words, "Beauty consists in absolute balance." "Beauty" reappeared in the pristine enchantment of pure forms, forms in the truly noble materials of marble and polished bronze. In his magnificent isolation from time, Brancusi never realized that he was interpreting his era's highest artistic ideals.

Like so many others, he had begun with a *tour de force*, a showpiece of academic virtuosity, but the first decisive work related to his ultimate destiny as a creative artist was, as we have said, *The Kiss*, which he carved in 1908 for the Montparnasse cemetery. Here he had found his style, a style that owed nothing to past civilizations and was repeated in the *Arch* (1917). The world of primitive forms, revealed by avant-garde sculptors moved by the overriding influence of African sculpture, found its elemental simplicity of conception, purged of all ritual or magic overtones, in the work of Brancusi. It was an original, authentic world, directly present, which kept the aggressive innocence of its origins in spite of stylistic perfection.

The Prodigal Son (1914), *Witch* (1916), *Endless Column* (1918), *Chimera* (1918), and *Adam and Eve* of 1921 (figure 4) are fantasies inspired by memories of remote traditions. And *King of Kings* (1918) is a figure-object, a Surrealist figure out of some impossible game of chess, expressed with bizarre, ironic humor. Wood and stone, marble and bronze determined the character of certain images, for Brancusi had discovered the expressive values of materials worked with a patience that sprang from a love of durability.

His longing for perfection is even better expressed in his more intensely spiritual sculptures, *Child's Head* (1906), *Sleeping Muse* (1909–10), *Prometheus* (1911), *Newborn Child* (1915), which mark the successive stages of a severe process of formal simplification. The final bareness of imagery, in the absolute purity of a synthesis that embraces all other works along the same lines, is achieved in *Sculpture for the Blind Man* (1924). Brancusi has been accused of attributing aesthetic values to pebbles polished by the sea, as if they were *objets trouvés* (found objects). And indeed, *Sculpture for the Blind Man* may remind one of a pebble or an egg, but in this case the reference concerns a form conceived in accordance with the demanding laws of purism. Such a demand is historically justified as a reaction against the descriptive naturalism of the nineteenth century with its bourgeois statuary, and also by an enriched culture that invaded the fields of archaeology and ethnography to add new elements to the history of art. In this reformulation of culture, aimed at crystalliz-ing his "archaic" style, Brancusi had a neighbor, pupil, and master: Modigliani.

But how did contemporary society react when faced with Brancusi's austere conceptions, with his love for beauty translated in terms of the most modern purism? Hardly at all, for in fact, Brancusi had no contact with society as such, and his real public consisted of other artists. Only a small body of faithful followers in France and the United States collected his works and brought them to general attention through museum collections and exhibits. Today Brancusi's works are regarded as "classics": his "time" is that of the Tibetan sages, immeasurable — the time of men who do not reveal themselves in the moment, who are always beyond the present.

Brancusi's art gives one a sense of eternity, and his artist-followers understood this, especially in *Sleeping Muse, Prometheus*, and *Sculpture for the Blind Man*.

The myth of pure form was to become a reality in modern sculpture (Arp, Moore, Pevsner, Chauvin, Béothy, Gilioli, Lipsi, Hajdu): a primordial reality, set against Cubism, Surrealism, or even the works of the great traditional masters, who conceived stylistic purity in a totally different way.

Brancusi's aesthetic ideal did not crystallize with *Sleeping Muse* but developed through his later works, year after year, to *Seal* and *Dove in Flight* by way of the series of Birds in Space which seem to be soaring into infinite space in a positively supernatural leap.

No cultural regression halted the course of Brancusi's creative cycle. Yet cultural regression is liable to be the end point for certain varieties of system-ridden purism pushed beyond their true historical periods. But Brancusi never made an academic dogma out of the perfection of his forms in relation to the quality of their materials. Everything in him was real and spontaneous, whether he was cutting wood to make a table or chair, polishing the marble fish, or, like a good mason, carving the pilasters of the *Gate* (1935–37) in Târgu-Jiu in Romania. Everything becomes poetry in the work of this great craftsman, who defended himself with candor and malice, violence and irony. He carried in himself an overpoweringly strong love for nature, combined with a cosmic faith, that saved him from anguish and the fear of death.

As Arp said of the *Cock*:

Le coq de Brancusi est une scie de joie.

Ce coq scie le jour de l'arbre de la lumière....

Only a poet of Arp's caliber could penetrate so deeply into Brancusi's world.

A very different, if not resolutely opposed, picture is provided by the development of the other "great" of modern sculpture: Pablo Picasso (1881–).

African sculpture, which out of deference to the principles of traditional art had always been relegated to ethnographical museums, began to appear in the shop windows of the Rue de Rennes at the turn of the century, perhaps as a result of the fashion for the exotic launched by Gauguin, which had gained momentum from the increasing interest in non-European art. This vague interest led to many revolutionary discoveries and a consequent enrichment, in depth and breadth, of art appreciation.

Matisse and Picasso discovered African art in those Parisian shops which contrive to collect and display the newest, strangest, most unexpected things, giving the public the impression of having made the discovery themselves. Fetishes and masks, statuettes, and everyday objects from the various regions of the "Dark Continent," as Africa was then called, revealed a magical world of forms, mysterious, cruel, and bloodthirsty, of unknown rites, cults, and beliefs, often relics of civilizations now dead and forgotten.

One had to learn to see inside these forms and images which represented sculpture in its true original state, in its natural, uncontaminated expressiveness, free from any influence of Mediterranean artistic cultures. And in order to learn to see one had to be blessed with extreme freedom of vision, whether innate, as in Picasso's case, or rationally achieved, as with Matisse. Yet, both created on the basis of African art the fundamental premises for a new conception of sculpture.

19

The venerable Maillol, ever faithful to his original Greek ideal had, nevertheless, shrewdly guessed the character of African sculpture. "One must aim at synthesis," he said, "like these African sculptors who reduce twenty forms into one." This definitive synthesis, which eliminated every superfluous descriptive element to leave the work charged only with pure plastic energy, gave Picasso fresh impetus toward the barbaric inventiveness of the distorted masks that must have served as studies for the famous *Les Demoiselles d'Avignon* of 1907 — though Picasso himself claimed never to have seen any African sculpture before painting this work.

Be that as it may, this contact with Negro sculpture gave rise to a new cycle in his work, very different from the Blue and Rose periods, which took concrete form in the *Woman's Head* of 1909 (figure 5) with a highly inventive sculptural vision that owes nothing to convention. (The constant danger of "cultural" art is precisely that it risks inventing nothing.)

In its first phases, Cubist sculpture was the plastic interpretation of painterly sculpture: of the analysis, decomposition, and reconstruction of the object that are to be found in the paintings of Picasso and Braque. To find its own forms in terms of true Cubist aesthetics, sculpture had to await the experiments of Archipenko and Zadkine, and, most of all, Laurens and Lipchitz.

After paying homage to Rodin and Medardo Rosso (*Harlequin*), Picasso created, in his *Woman's Head,* an archetype that was to inspire Boccioni and Martini; it is composed of deep hollows, which replace volume with void and empty shadow, spreading structural chiaroscuro effects over the mass so as to create an illusion of relief. In fact, this work touched off a new type of vision in modern sculpture. On the other hand, in *Harlequin* Picasso remained faithful to the refined idiom of his Rose Period paintings, modeling the head with a *sfumato* almost reminiscent of Rosso.

The Glass of Absinthe and *Construction* are composed of wooden elements and colored plaster, and have no precedent in the history of art, for they interpret the principles of Cubism down to the last letter. (Picasso has denied the existence of any such doctrine.) It is certain that these two works by Picasso play a key role in the formulation of a Cubist plastic language.

The sculpture of Derain and Matisse, of Dufy and Braque had other origins — neolithic statuettes or pre-Phidian Grecian work, Mediterranean votive figurines, and Aztec or Mayan sculpture — yielding archaic elements that suggested a fine range of formal motifs, unorthodox when seen from a traditional standpoint, but nonetheless still within the domain of "cultural" art.

Picasso soon worked out his interest for "constructions" and relief collages that recalled the cutouts of children's model theaters; he forgot Cubism and threw himself into the neoclassical adventure and the rather ironic sculptures that represent the distortion of the "ideally beautiful" into the "expressively ugly" — within the limits, however, of continual plastic invention. Picasso is a magician who never fails to work the most unexpected transformations on materials and subjects, so that they seem invented afresh.

His iron trellises, inspired by Gonzalez, soldered iron incorporating everyday objects, become totemic apparitions when photographed by night in an overgrown garden. The *Useless Monuments* which never got beyond the paper stage (reproduced in *Cahiers d'Art*) could serve as monuments to our times, but we shall never see them in a French city square. Many have imitated them, but along the wrong lines.

In 1943, with a bicycle seat and handlebars, Picasso invented a bull's head. His magical imagination transforms everything — commonplace objects as well as the human form — into something else. Maillol and Despiau were still alive then, but they could not have shared in the games of the great conjurer, in his amusement at absurd combinations of objects and figures.

Picasso has to work, work at all costs, inventing and interpreting, drawing on his inexhaustible vein of "inventions," for his art depends on action. But to judge Picasso only on the basis of his object metamorphoses would be to overlook the naturalistic side of his art: *Cock* (1932), *Cat* (1944), *Man with Lamb* of 1944 (Plate XX), *Goat* (1950), and *Monkey* (1951). No one has penetrated deeper into the spirit and character of animals than Picasso in his sculpted "Natural History." Even in these works, with their almost symbolic archetypal faithfulness to their subjects, Picasso has incorporated objects so brilliantly revalued that they become active parts of some of the most lively figure sculpture of the century. As in much of Picasso's work, the relationship with nature is expressed in a total participation that springs impetuously from the very roots of things.

When Picasso went to live in Vallauris, his inventive instinct was aroused once more by the new adventure of ceramics, the discovery of a technique new to him, which forced him to work even more intensively than before, feverishly consuming themes and motifs inspired by reality or visual memory. He rediscovered his Mediterranean origins, not through naturalistic regression — which would have been impossible for him in any case — but through the myths and figures of a time in which he felt completely at home.

The *Man with Lamb* is a figure from Paleo-Christian art, given new life in a very free modern interpretation as a symbol of the simplicity of the soul and the love of peace. Picasso made it as a monument, and it now stands in the main square of Vallauris among the trees under the strong southern sun: children clamber over it — it belongs to everyone. In this way *Man with Lamb* has been transformed into an "active" monument, like Rodin's *Balzac*, over and above the intrinsic aesthetic value of the work.

But for Picasso this was only one of the countless moments into which his artistic life can be divided. Another moment gave us the *Woman's Head* of 1941 (Plate XXI), conceived in the neoclassical spirit whose roots can be traced back to the artist's travels in Italy in 1917; the work was later placed in front of the church of Saint Germain des Prés and dedicated to the memory of Guillaume Apollinaire, who had lived only two blocks away on the Boulevard Saint Germain. The same neoclassical spirit is revealed in graphic works, from the *Centaur and Woman* of 1920 to the engravings for Ovid's *Metamorphoses* of 1930, which are distinguished by a cleanness of line and purity of imagery that are to be found only in the mythological inventions of the Leucadians or the rhythmic calligraphy of Attic vases. With the *Classical Head* of 1921 Picasso had created the prototype of the 1941 *Head*, which might belong to some Juno of the Augustan age, for, in spite of all its divine impassiveness, it is still florid and slightly animal. Picasso, like Stravinsky, often returned to fanciful interpretations of the Classical world in the spirit of an ironic, critical present.

In fact, the 1941 *Head*, which is a monument to the poetry of Apollinaire, mingles nature and culture in an image which is at once Classical and contemporary. After all, is it not true that Apollinaire was an ultramodern poet who continued the most limpid traditions of French poetry? Besides, in Picasso's work even ambiguity often transforms itself into enigmatic poetry.

And so these two monuments, which seemed destined to be shut away in the hermetic world of avant-garde art and cut off from the participation and approval of anyone, let alone city dwellers, became vitally important realities accepted by whole communities, key elements in a social environment of which they have become the most faithful and elevated symbols. It is worth noting here that Picasso has always conceived his sculptures for real space, whether this space is a public square, a beach, a forest clearing, or a reflecting pool. Once in this space, the sculptures acquire their true dimensions.

In 1957 Picasso conjured up the cutout *Bathers*, similar to the metal banners or cocks that used to serve as weather vanes. These cutouts, which could easily be used for an ironical game of Aunt Sally, were exhibited at Kassel in 1959 in a large pool of water — their most fitting environment and space. This is one of the last metamorphoses in the passage from sculpture to object that Picasso has brought about with his open-minded freedom of invention, in which there is just enough implied playfulness to render even the most extravagant caprices of his fancy acceptable. His *Bathers* are the targets for an intellectual target practice, the objects on which the artist's endless creative inspiration unleashes itself. What other devilries has the old magician of Malaga up his sleeve in his perpetual battle against time?

Picasso sculpted the *Warrior* (1933) with the plumed helmet of Homeric heroes, and his *Skull* (1943) is a homage to tragic, funereal Mexico. One is a caricature of power and war, the other a caricature of death. Nothing is safe from the artist's pitiless gaze: irony and drama mingle in the infinite variety of life. He is as totally committed to the game as to denunciation, on condition that every element should be or become the substance of life. Living, in this sense, comes to imply moral judgment and an undertaking to turn every motif into an instrument of poetry.

In its boundless inventive richness, Picasso's work never falls to the level of mediocrity or mechanical repetition. As an inventor of Cubism, he created Cubist works, but never followed a rigid method that might have led him to monotonous solutions dependent on a facile relationship of cause and effect. The basic difference between Picasso and the Cubists proper consists precisely in this: in his complete liberty before certain problems and certain stylistic systems. Picasso always invents — his strength lies in the continual resources of his imagination and his anti-systematic temperament.

He is not therefore responsible for Cubist Mannerism, which is to be detected in the excessive method and overfaithful adherence to system in the otherwise noteworthy works of Archipenko, Zadkine, Lipchitz, and Csaky.

Along with Brancusi, Arp, Laurens, Picasso, and Pevsner, Julio Gonzalez (1876–1942) is one of the most important sculptors of the century. The key dates in his life are: 1900, when he moved from Barcelona to Paris; 1927, when he gave up painting

Figure 5 - Pablo Picasso (1881-): *Woman's Head*, bronze, 1909.

to devote himself exclusively to sculpture; 1929, when he initiated Picasso into the techniques of ironwork; and the period from 1929 to 1934, when, after a long series of experiments and essays, he succeeded in producing totally abstract sculpture.

From his earliest childhood, Gonzalez had learned to work with metals — his father and grandfather were goldsmiths — but the craftsman had to wait many years before emerging as an artist, an artist who invented new forms that explain a large part of modern sculpture as far as Chillida or even César (cf. *Character: the Giraffe* dated 1934).

Gonzalez' history as a craftsman and painter is of little importance: the sculptor emerges suddenly, between 1927 and 1930, in full maturity and in full possession of his technical means. In the early stages, one can still trace influences of Negro sculpture (the Masks) and Cubism (the Heads and Still Lifes). But the elementary transfiguration of naturalistic content in the small figure of *Don Quixote* (1929), composed of pieces of iron directly welded together (Gonzalez had learned to use the oxhydrogen welder in 1916–17 when he was working in the Renault factory, and in this, too, he is an absolute pioneer), anticipates the series of figures executed between 1931 and 1933, which are reduced to pure graphic outlines dominated by very lively rhythm.

His Faces are aesthetic Cubist masks with impenetrable expressions, sometimes formulated in terms of an abstract structure, imitated and repeated thereafter *ad nauseam*. These Faces have a superstructure of planes calculated to accentuate the depth of shadow and the sense of mystery. On the other hand, the iron sculptures are cleanly outlined in a space which they reconstruct, in accordance with Gonzalez' ambition, in the ideal trajectory of movement. *Motherhood* (1931), *Standing Figure* (1932), and *Angel* of 1933 (Plate XXII) oppose *stasis*, almost hieratic immobility, to the obsessional rhythm of *Prayer* (1932) and *Disheveled Dancer* (1934). The sculptor's fantastic inspiration is best shown in *The Dream* (1931), *Large Horn* (1932–34), *Woman Combing Her Hair* (1933), *Giraffe* (1934), *Small Egyptian Torso* (1934), and the two versions of *Seated Woman* (1935).

Picasso's bizarre fetishes have much in common with these sculptures, which, with the crudeness of their female profiles cut like scythe blades and set with squares of sheet metal into a framework of soldered iron rods, have been likened to instruments of torture, executioners' axes and swords. It is easy to see them as symbols of a certain Spanish sadism, although Gonzalez disliked such symbols and allusions. The figures anticipate Picasso's *Bathers* and, as we have said, seem directly descended from inn signs and weathercocks. The nature of iron determined the sculptor's exciting vision. Gonzalez transformed the iron, bending it into something significant, expressive, and new in a freshly conquered space.

In *Motherhood*, a theme to which the sculptor often returned, and *Small Egyptian Torso* (1934), this period gave us motifs that have inspired countless modern sculptors, from Consagra to Chevignier. Then, from 1934 to 1937, Gonzalez resumed contact with the tragic reality of Spain in the series of figures of the women of Montserrat, culminating in *La Montserrat* in the Amsterdam Museum, and *Mask of Screaming Woman*, two images of the same moment: the first is monumental, showing a woman who gives an impression of solemn, irresistible strength, while the second expresses pain and terror, a mask of the desperate protest of a free spirit. Eight years later,

24

with the *Head of Montserrat* of 1942 (Plate XXIII), Gonzalez protested again, against other, more human horrors and tragedies. His last sculpture, a fragment of what was to be a work of monumental dimensions, represents a standing Montserrat woman, more human than the Amsterdam figure, sadder and more tragic.

In 1934 Gonzalez sculpted *The Kiss*, a head in the form of a medieval helmet, which could be the archetype recalled later in works by Henry Moore. But the essential transfiguring force of Gonzalez' vision reaches its ultimate consolidation in the *The Great Sickle* (1936), *Gothic Man* (1937), *Dancer with Flower* (1938), *Cactus Man I* (1939—40), and the bronze *Cactus Man II* (1938).

The expressive potential of iron as a "modern" material is affirmed through Gonzalez' flawless technical skill, in the very modernity of his artistic conception and creation. *Cactus Man I* is the most complete synthesis of reality and abstraction achieved by the artist, with a stylistic rigor verging on the absolute.

If Gonzalez taught Picasso the techniques of ironwork, Picasso in return gave him valuable advice, setting him on the road toward freedom from the hindrances of traditional influences, toward complete independence of vision. Indeed, in *Cactus Man* Gonzalez had emulated Picasso's open-minded imaginative freedom in the metamorphosis of human into vegetable forms. His art contains many of the most original discoveries of the time, always on a Surrealist plane, but Gonzalez was always rather apart from contemporary artistic experiments, if only because very few others could have "invented" with iron outside the limits of then current cultural structures.

Pablo Gargallo (1881—1934) had also worked in iron from 1913 onward, but he drew his inspiration from Picasso's painting, Negro masks, and Modigliani's heads to produce naturalistic representation, in spite of the addition of ornamental elements. Gargallo cut away his iron silhouette along traditionally inspired lines, then welded other iron elements onto these cutouts to simulate the relief that in sculpture is normally achieved with full volumes and voids.

In *Antinous* (1932) the procedure serves to animate the surface with emphatic chiaroscuro effects. In *Harlequin with Flute* of 1933 (Plate XXIV) the sheet elements are cut to correspond to the muscles of the arms and legs and the features of the face. The holes project Cubist-inspired patterns on the plane surfaces. But the voids that replace full volumes, the concavities that take the place of convexities are, in these two sculptures, only parts that add nothing to the inventiveness of the whole work, which depends too closely on Picasso's formal repertory.

Gargallo's finest sculpture is the stone head of Picasso, which shows acutely perceptive interpretation of the sitter's character, but bears no relation to the mannered, decorative elegance of the figures cut in sheet metal. Ultimately, Gargallo must be classed among those interpreters and assimilators of styles who form the substratum of the artistic world, alongside the great movements in twentieth-century avant-garde art. But often the minor figures add to our understanding of the more important ones.

Often classed with Picasso for reasons of style, Raymond Duchamp-Villon (1876—1918), who precedes Gonzalez chronologically, can be linked with Boccioni as one of the precursors of avant-garde sculpture. He drew his first inspiration from Rodin, as can be seen from his *Woman's Torso* (1907) and *Youth's Torso* (1910). The most conclusive work of this first period is a bust of Baudelaire, displaying an elevated style that is without parallel in the portrait sculpture of the period (Plate XXV). The work is conceived and executed on the spiritual scale of certain Egyptian statues, and at the same time it is defined in the immediacy of an intensely expressive interpretation: an immortal Baudelaire shown in his most characteristic human reality, a true Baudelaire remote in the fixed concentration of his gaze. Duchamp-Villon completely fulfilled his aim in this head of the poet-bonze, and showed far greater boldness than in *The Lovers* of 1913, which many critics consider as a more or less Cubist low relief, or the 1913 *Seated Woman*, which could better be compared with a "metaphysical" manikin.

While *The Lovers* seems inspired by Maillol and *Seated Woman* by Rodin, the two sculptures reveal a determination to go beyond pure and simple representation, to reach another plastic reality in which each form tends toward its own emphatic expressive value, in spite of the sculptor's evident intention of giving the works a purist unity of style.

In *Baudelaire* Duchamp-Villon had proposed a type of "modern" style, but since "modern" was identified at that time with formal dynamics, we have to wait for the famous *Horse's Head* of 1914 (Plate XXVI) for a clearer, more precise formulation of this style. In 1912 the Futurist painters had exhibited for the first time in Paris. Marcel Duchamp had drawn inspiration from their documentary demonstrations, then outstripped them with the cinematographic description of movement in *Nude Descending a Staircase* which, with *Horse's Head*, is one of the seminal documents of the modern avant garde. In April 1913, Boccioni exhibited some Futurist sculptures in Paris, among them *Unique Forms of Continuity in Space* which projected muscular contractions and dilatations into space with unusual visual candor. Duchamp-Villon studied attentively the way in which this work resolved the problems of movement.

According to Alfred Barr, Duchamp-Villon's *Horse's Head* goes beyond Boccioni, "not so much in kinetic illusionism as, certainly, in dynamic strength." Werner Hofmann expresses the same opinion in his *Plastik des 20. Jahrhunderts*, noting that the *Horse's Head* shows the development of "a determined expressiveness that is difficult to explain in terms of the Cubist and Futurist concepts."

But what is this sculpture, with its "dynamic strength" opposed to the "static strength" of *Baudelaire*? Before attempting to reply, it is well to remember that in 1912 Duchamp-Villon had studied the possibility of applying Cubist forms to architecture and in 1913 exhibited his *Cubist House* in the Salon d'Automne. It is also significant that he had studied the problems of the Cubist aesthetic in the basic "texts," with the same application he later devoted to the study of Futurist material.

The structure of the *Horse's Head* presupposed knowledge of Léger's work of the mechanist Cubist period. In fact, it is composed of the fragments of a mechanism reassembled in a pseudoanalytical order. The world of Léger is transformed by the creative enlightenment of the sculptor into an autonomous form — which many people have attributed to the rigorous rationality of the artist. In fact, this rationality is only superficial in the construction of *Horse's Head*, which does not depend on mathematical formulas, as do certain works of Gabo and Pevsner. The inner dynamics of *Horse's Head* stem from poetic invention, more mysterious and less fully demonstrated than in Boccioni's *Unique Forms*; in this way the plastic energy emitted by the mechanical device is on its way to becoming something else, just as in Picasso's magical manipulations. Its leaping movement embraces the absurd mechanisms that replace the moving muscles.

Duchamp-Villon died in 1918 at the early age of 42, so that his reputation as a precursor, totally independent of the Futurist and Cubist aesthetics at the climactic moment of a feverish collective search for a new conception of art, remained founded entirely on *Horse's Head*. What else might Duchamp-Villon have done had he not died so young? The question is not altogether senseless, given the basic premise of a work valid in its own terms as well as in those of its time, while still audaciously aimed at the future. However, it must remain unanswered, for history is not built on hypotheses.

Fortunately, beside Duchamp-Villon, there were two other artists who can provide a possible answer to this question, for they demonstrated, through their development, the stylistic solutions implicit in the teachings and experiments of Cubist art: Henri Laurens (1885–1956) and Jacques Lipchitz (1891–). Laurens' contribution to the development of Cubist sculpture is of the most vital importance. Today, as Zervos observed in *Cahiers d'Art* in 1930, it is difficult to realize just how great was the enthusiasm of young people meeting with the works of Braque and Picasso, which were the boldest experiments ever seen in the history of art. "The Cubist experiment could not fail to captivate young, vigorous imaginations; it was as if an unhoped-for vision had made its appearance, as if a new consciousness had been created, bringing with it a completely unprecedented conception of art." Certainly, in a period dominated by the elegant, aristocratic international style of Boldini, Lavery, and Besnard and the anecdotal naturalism modeled on the already remote examples of Meissonnier and Fortuny, Cubist art must have appeared incomprehensible or downright mad — not only to the high society that then dominated intellectual and political life, but also to many young people incapable of recognizing Cubism as an artistic reality of fundamental importance to the history of modern art.

From 1911 on, Laurens was a close friend of Braque, Gris, Picasso, and Léger. His *Plastics* in polychromed wood and plaster, similar in many ways to the Futurist mixed-media objects, are straightforward transpositions into relief of Cubist still lifes of the analytical and synthetic periods. Laurens' experiments were limited to the still life, that is, to the analysis of volumes decomposed to reveal their real structure and recomposed in an order that theoretically should be rational, but, now that time has elapsed, appears to be an entirely personal invention.

The illusionism of the constructions was made all the more evident by the coloring of the various wood, plaster, and cardboard elements, which were used precisely as they had been in collage and painting, so that the constructions included printed words, labels from wine bottles, glasses, fruit bowls, all the objects and instruments from the Cubist repertory. Cubism limits the field of analytical research to a few categories of objects: the most poor and banal elements taken from everyday *petit-bourgeois* existence are adopted as material for extremely lucid structural and compositional research. The guitar and the bottle take the place of Polyclitus' nude.

Henri Laurens' methodical study of these models between 1915 and 1918 was to lead from analytical decomposition to the synthesis of more abstract Cubism in the works of 1918: *Glass and Bottle, Musical Instrument,* and *Fruit Bowl.* In 1951, in a conversation with Yvon Taillandier, Laurens appraised these first experiments of his in a historical context, and said: "During the Cubist period we were only interested in the object as such. Our only problem was the search for pure sensation, the sensation of volume and our search for this volume. . . . We all thought along the same lines. But we could hardly spend the rest of our lives making *papiers collés.*"

In fact, in 1919 Laurens had already proposed a more specifically sculptural solution for Cubist composition with his *Man with Pipe* and, the following year with *Guitar*, carved in stone with the same plastic vigor that later characterized the many female nudes executed in accordance with the principles he had clearly grasped and expressed in the reality of a style distinguished by its powerful relief and life. "Before being a representation of anything, my sculpture is a plastic act, or more exactly, a series of plastic events, products of my imagination, responses to the demands of the construction."

And in *Man with Pipe* (Plate XXVII) Laurens' sculpture becomes a plastic act that opens the way for other plastic acts in an autonomous relationship with space. Until then, Cubist constructions had depended completely on the existence of a real or imaginary backdrop which laid down their basically pictorial space. Instead, to use Laurens' words, "sculpture is essentially a possession of space, the construction of an object in full volumes and voids, their alternation and contrast, their constant and reciprocal tension and ultimately, the equilibrium between them. The happy solution of the particular problem and the relative success of the work correspond to the intensity of this formal composition. The work must be static for all its movement; then space will radiate out from it and be composed in terms of the sculpture."

These are very general thoughts, but necessary for an understanding of the sculptor's development, especially after 1926, when he abandoned polychromy and the more specifically Cubist thematics. The most convincing products of this new phase of Laurens' activity are the *Seated Woman* of 1932 (Plate XXIX) and *Torso* of 1935 which, in spite of their small dimensions, already herald the monumentality of the nudes, from the *Bathers* of 1947 to the *Large Musician* of 1950. The plastic mass is defined by the full volumes and the decisive synthesis of the outline: the sculpture truly constitutes a "possession of space" and is indeed static despite the rhythm that animates its inner structures. The typical stylistic traits of Cubism are henceforth assimilated and integrated into the monumental conception of Laurens' sculptures. Hollows and volumes, full and empty spaces alternate harmoniously in the concentric development of the organic sculptural composition, delimited by solemn, generous curves. *The Farewell* of 1941 (Plate XXVIII), *Night* (1943), and *Large Archangel* (1948) are among the most conscientious of Laurens' mature works, modeled in clay and cast in bronze, like antique sculptures. And the relationship between the quality of forms and the material employed is resolved in a perfect unity of style.

The 1950 *Large Musician* (Plate XXX) is far removed from the spirit of experimental Cubism: it belongs rather to a type of modern statuary that embraces the ideological demands and formal conquests of its time. The same could be said of Lipchitz' latest baroque sculptures, beside which the Cubist-inspired works appear set in a closed historical period.

This is not a case of regression, but, on the contrary, a development that could never have taken place without the initial shock of Cubism and the freedom it won. This evolution has taken place without ambiguity or stylistic compromise, aided by the culture most sympathetic to the spirit of modern artists, and reflects in its choices a desire for the stylistic purity discovered in the works of African sculptors and archaic societies. To establish a meaningful comparison for a fair evaluation of modern sculpture, it should be enough to consider how Maillol and Laurens, living and working in virtually the same historical context, resolved the influence of archaic art in their respective work.

"I want to arrive at sculpture pure as crystal," said Jacques Lipchitz (1891–) in October 1909 when he arrived in Paris from his native Lithuania. This was the aim of many sculptors who flocked to Paris from all the corners of the earth, attracted by a climate of intellectual fervor and spiritual freedom. Lipchitz settled in Paris in 1912 and met Juan Gris in 1916. With the guiding advice of that artist, whose theoretical and moral rigor never faltered, he was able to continue the Cubist experiment. Yet, in his complicated constructions of planes he never abandoned the basic figuration that served as a model for the compound mannerism that flowered in the shade of the major personalities of the modern avant garde. Cubist sculpture did not undergo the same coherent development as Cubist painting, of which, as we have already said, it was generally a three-dimensional interpretation. Even Lipchitz, in his still lifes of 1918, 1919, and 1921, interpreted the paintings of Gris, equaling the Spaniard's geometrical rigor in composition.

In 1915 Lipchitz sculpted and cast in bronze a *Head* which can be used to trace the process of abstraction that he followed with a view to enclosing the head and its spatial setting in monumental architectural forms, simplifying all planes. This was Lipchitz' most daring attempt at giving coherent construction and stylistic unity to the Cubist plasticity. In another sculpture, *Scholar* (1915), he aimed at reducing the human figure to a few geometrical outlines bound together in compliance with a facile model of abstract synthesis. The result is an object, not a sculpture, a childish ornament.

Sailor with Guitar (Plate XXXI) is an early example of the most typical Cubist iconography, which Lipchitz continued in *Woman with Guitar* (1917–18), *Guitar Player* (1918), *Pierrot with Clarinet* (1919), *Figure* (1919), the two versions of *Man with Clarinet* (1920), and *Man with Guitar* (1920). The theme of the guitar players reappears in various forms in 1925, when the first hints of baroque tendencies can be seen, and 1926, when the figure is reduced to a skeleton of lines represented by thin, wavy strips of material and very fine, twisted cords fused together in the void, which suggest the volume of the torso. In this case, too, the rhythm is baroque, but the sculpture avoids becoming a simple object. However, the decorative tendency in his stylization of forms becomes more accentuated in *Musical Instruments* (1924) and *Ploumanach* (1926), overflowing into excess and downright pleonasm.

The surreal aspect of images inspired by the enigmatic idols of primitive African and Oceanic peoples is another characteristic of twentieth-century avant-garde art. Lipchitz renders this aspect even more obscure and mysterious in his *Figure* of 1926–30 (Plate XXXII) which interprets a nostalgia for the primitive state and magical arts, in irrational reaction against an overorganized, technical world. And the 1932 *Head*, hollowed out like a money box with a wavy horizontal opening, is raw and primitive like the work of some prehistoric potter, one of the countless modes, so popular in modern art, of expressing rebellion against the overmechanized civilization that has destroyed man's taste for simple things. Moore alludes to this sculpture and the Gonzalez helmet in his series of *Warrior Heads*.

The Couple (1928–30) is the exact antithesis of the 1926 *Guitar Player*, by virtue of the savage violence of the image animated by a sensual rhythm: a contorted, convulsive composition, with a strange baroque quality superimposed on the original Cubist structure. This road toward a new type of figuration leads to the two *Prometheus* paintings of 1936 and 1943, the *Song of the Vowels* of 1930–32 (Plate XXXIII), *The Rape of Europa* of 1938 (Plate XXXIV), *Theseus* of 1942, and *Sacrifice* of 1947, in which dramatic tension acquires a rhythm pushed to its extreme limits by the impetus of the gesture, that once more suggests comparisons with the flying angels and wind-blown robes set in the theatrical space of baroque altars and fountains.

The sketches for *Prometheus* and *Song of the Vowels* represent this animation of figures linked together in the same upward rush — which in itself has a symbolic meaning. Thus, Lipchitz grew out of the Cubist period, finding a new stylistic balance in the world of baroque fantasy, inspired by mythological themes or his own desire to create a new mythology of force and violence.

In 1941 Lipchitz left France for New York, where, during the last few years, he has executed a long series of monumental works, culminating in *Notre Dame de Liesse* for the Church of Assy in Haute-Savoie. His most recent experiments have aimed, in complete opposition to the static Cubist compositions, at fixing increasingly more dynamic movement in the forms of virtually abstract expressionism. This is the extreme limit of the baroque situation, well interpreted in the sketch for *Loie Fuller* (1956), shown in the important retrospective of the artist's work in Amsterdam in 1958. With the expressive exaggeration of raging, disarticulated, impetuous movement, the structural freedom of this sketch relates it to contemporary expressionist works.

In his first nudes, Alexander Archipenko (1887–) drew generously on Art Nouveau, whose refined, decorative cadences allowed him to transform even the Classical undertones of *Black Torso* (1909) into an object of considerable formal elegance. Like so many others of his time, Archipenko left Russia to settle in Paris in 1908. From 1910 to 1920 he drew his greatest inspiration from the Cubist aesthetic, especially in two important works: the *Head* of 1913 and *Boxing Match* of 1914 (figure 6).

It cannot be claimed that his slender figures have a truly Cubist structure. In the Venice Biennale of 1920, Archipenko's loose-limbed dancing works — some of which were described as sculpture-paintings — in plaster, bronze, terracotta, wood, or metal, might have been taken as figure studies for a ballet and, in some cases, modern interpretations of Greco-Roman motifs. He contrived to bestow airy lightness on practically bodiless images, which have been likened to the figures of the then fashionable Ballets Russes. But the authentic Cubist figures are still those that Picasso created for Satie's ballet *Parade*. These archetypes of Picasso's, which opened the way for interpreting a whole new range of figures and objects in a Cubist idiom, along with Duchamp-Villon's *Seated Woman*, provided sources from which Archipenko drew inspiration for his own expertly executed versions. *Medrano* (1914) comes shortly before Laurens' constructions, as does *Boxing Match*, which is without doubt Archipenko's most seminal contribution to modern sculpture. In 1923, he left for the United States, and from then on his works showed an increasingly decadent formal

30

Figure 6 - Alexander Archipenko (1887-): *Boxing Match*, painted plaster, 1914.

elegance that brought them closer and closer to Art Nouveau objects: it is a strange turn, as if he had returned to his first sources.

Ossip Zadkine (1890–) arrived in Paris in 1909 and immediately made the acquaintance of Lipchitz and Archipenko, among others. He too arrived when Cubism was in full swing, and he adopted the movement with innocent enthusiasm, attempting to interpret its most characteristic forms.

One of his first Cubist-inspired works is *Female Figures* of 1918 (Plate XXXV), in which the frontal representation is broken up in an attempt to turn the form around and show both sides simultaneously by means of several inventive devices. But as sculpture it is too obvious, too closely linked to the theoretical principles of Cubist composition, as if the craftsman Zadkine had been enmeshed in acquired formulas which were to serve him only as an experiment, a point of departure for development along wholly different lines.

It is difficult to follow Zadkine's career, which proceeds in leaps and bounds, with returns to Cubism and Expressionism, restful decorative pauses, attentive naturalism (*Portrait of Van Gogh*), and, above all, dramatic excursions into the baroque. His progress is a flux and reflux of search and certainty, of happy inspiration and relapse, a continual alternation of passages — from surfaces modeled in the manner of marble to those done in the technique more natural to him, that of wood. Like Brancusi, Zadkine made not only sculpture, but also carved tables and chairs in the rough style of the peasants of old Russia.

His sculptures, often hacked or hollowed out in the middle, following the example of Gargallo or Lipchitz, use the characteristic iconography of the avant-garde, with a great variety of gestures and attitudes that are often tormented and rhetorical. Harlequins, dancers, masks, and musicians alternate with mythological figures, for Zadkine believes in a slightly ingenuous mythology in which every hero can become, through imaginative transposition, *The Poet* or *Orpheus* or *The Maenads* (Plate XXXVI).

Following his true vocation, Zadkine prefers wood to marble or bronze. He cuts deeply into the material and often polychromes it, in accordance with a popular tradition that often leads him close to folk art, as in the dramatic *Pietà*. Zadkine is constantly faithful to the figures of his personal mythology, to which he has added Jarry, Apollinaire, and Van Gogh. A constellation of divinities seen through a severe realism, with occasional Cubist reminiscences: this is the dream world of Zadkine, who has never lost his attachment to nature and the land of his fathers. The work of his that is most closely bound up in the expressive magniloquence of the gesture is his *Monument Commemorating the Destruction of Rotterdam* (1953–54) placed in its natural space, in which the truth of its protest rises like a cry of moral indignation. In other works, such as *Homage to Bach* (1932), he cultivates his decorative taste to the point of imitating music in a curvilinear interpretation of rococo. Zadkine is a true master, in the fullest sense of the word. Countless pupils have passed through his studio or his classes in the Grande Chaumière to learn the craft of which the craftsman-artist possesses the poetic secret.

In the wake of Zadkine, Lipchitz, Laurens, and Archipenko, another artist, Joseph Csaky (1888–), came to Paris in 1908 and accepted the principles of Cubism. His steles and reliefs, for the most part conserved in the Kröller-Müller Museum, Otterlo, resume the themes already traced in the constructions of Laurens. Csaky is not an inventor like Picasso; his intellectualism and culture constitute an effective brake on any too-daring adventure and impose limits on any possible excesses. As it is, his sculptures always show aristocratic restraint and measure in the choice of marble or stone and in their flawless execution.

The youthful Cubist compositions, such as *Relief* of 1920 (Plate XXXVII), still make their presence felt in Csaky's later works, inspired by severe contemplation of Classical models, in particular Grecian sculpture. In his most recent works, for instance, *Variety* (1958), Csaky still remains close to the elegantly mannered, correct Cubist idiom of his *Standing Woman* of 1913 (Plate XXXVIII). Lately this skillful stonecarver has turned to bronze, hoping to find in this timeless traditional metal the material corresponding most closely to the Alexandrian period of antiquity and, in a more modern era, the art of Giambologna and his followers.

Though he subscribed to Cubism from the outset, Csaky, like Chauvin, stayed rather apart from the melee, cut off by his preference for solitude. Louis Chauvin (1889–) is on of the most self-effacing and least known of French artists, a furious worker, even in the early days when, as Joseph Bernard's assistant, he made figurative sculpture. However, apart from the usual academic techniques, Bernard had little to teach him, so Chauvin went his own way and soon faced the problems raised by Cubism. Since then, he has never ceased to perfect his own characteristic repertory, adapting it to the materials used, and showing a marked preference for rare woods and marbles worked with the same attention to finish to be found in many of Brancusi's works.

His sculptures are generally executed on a fairly small scale, constructed in accordance with the principles of symmetry and composed with absolute stylistic rigor, enclosed in lucid formal perfection. Chauvin's clear-cut images are the result of a Brancusi-inspired insistence on stylistic purity, but his constant, intellectualized formalism, based on geometrical abstraction, as in *Couple* of 1940 (Plate XXXIX), is sometimes softened by more agitated composition, for instance in his *Don Juan* of 1945 (Plate XL). He is to be considered with the masters of the modern avant garde as a figure worthy of respect, even though the hostile reactions to purism by later generations have left him with few followers.

Étienne Béothy (1897–1961) was one of the most active members of the second generation of avant-garde artists. A friend of Moholy-Nagy, he began his career as an architect in the Budapest School of Higher Study, and moved to Paris in 1925. He was a founder and vice-president from 1932 to 1936 of the Abstraction-Création group; in 1951 he collaborated with Léger and Le Corbusier on the review *Formes et Vie* and later founded the group Espace with André Bloc and Del Marie.

His brilliant career, distinguished by high intellectual and creative fervor, ran from a few figurative sculptures in the vein of Archipenko to later works in which the sinuous, enveloping movement is intended to express musical themes. The relationship between music and sculpture was systematically studied by Béothy, who hoped to find a basis and determining law for the work of art, corresponding to the Golden Section of the Renaissance. Musical inspiration is evident in his *Interlocking Rhythms* of 1937 (Plate XLI); and the importance of mathematical formulas shows in the elliptical development of the woodcarving *Vespa, op. 138* (1957). Béothy was a purist;

and, because of the rather cold and programmatic nature of his work, he must be classed with the Swiss sculptor Max Bill and the remarkable movement that, from 1932 to 1939, was dominated by geometrical abstraction and the theorems of spatial construction that had been applied to painting and architecture by Mondrian and Van Doesburg.

Georges Vantongerloo (1886–) attempted, in the name of the unity of art, to achieve a synthesis between sculpture and architecture. His puritan rigor led him to represent an equation: to construct objects on the basis of scientific formulas. His architectonic sculptures are constituted of structural elements, which could be said to have been prefabricated to the desired specifications, combined horizontally and vertically as in the famous Rietveld house in Utrecht. Vantongerloo belonged to the De Stijl group from its foundation in 1917, and to Abstraction-Création along with the most celebrated purists of the time — Gabo, Pevsner, Moholy-Nagy — working along the lines of Constructivism and Neoplasticism, and firmly convinced that these movements corresponded to the historical reality of the timidly launched machine age.

Vantongerloo has always remained first and foremost an architect, closer to architectural problems than to those of sculpture, which cannot, however plausible it may seem, be resolved with purely mathematical equations. His sculptures resemble scale models of buildings composed of polyvalent modular components, for example *Construction of Volumes* of 1918 (figure 7). Pushing methodical rigor beyond all its bounds, Vantongerloo was searching for a basic principle for art in the laws that govern the cosmos. In the course of cool-headed experiments from 1938 onward, he replaced the constructions of volumes with a series of compositions in steel wire drawn in the air, often holding plexiglass elements in the center of their complicated arabesques. However, these elements were never allowed to disturb the unity of the curved lines, seemingly inspired by automatic tracing. These elegant wire constructions, made to hang in space, can also be described as architectonic discoveries: one more attempt to create in inert space the creative forms of a truly artistic space.

Now Vantongerloo is one of the few survivors, along with the architect Van Rietveld, of the great Neoplastic adventure — which pervaded the entire world on the social and aesthetic levels and has left deeper, more durable marks than even Cubism itself.

With his Alsatian origins, Jean (Hans) Arp (1888–) unites two cultures and two natures, and maintains a completely objective attitude toward both. A distinguished poet in German, Arp is essentially a poet above all else, and he has contrived to live as a poet should, preserving himself from the vulgarity of men, their horrors and folly, during the first and second World Wars. In 1916, while the armies of Europe were intent on mutual decimation along the various fronts, Arp was in Zurich, painting and drawing, writing and carving reliefs; in the same year, along with Hugo Ball, Emmy Hennings, Richard Huelsenbeck, Marcel Janco, and Tristan Tzara, he founded the Dada movement, whose influence on the development of modern art was of capital importance. During the first years of the second World War, he lived in Grasse (1940–41) with Sophie Taueber, Sonia Delaunay, and Alberto Magnelli and published *Poèmes sans Prénoms*. Once more he drew and worked in total detachment from the tragic reality of war, close to his beloved Mediterranean, which he loved as he was later to love Greece; then he left Grasse for Switzerland, where his wife Sophie was to die on January 13, 1943. They had married in 1922 and in 1926 settled permanently in the house and studio in Meudon where the originals of many of Arp's works are preserved; Sophie's death left him in a state of inconsolable despair.

It is almost impossible to give even a rough outline of the immense body of work produced by Arp during more than sixty years of truly creative activity, even though, in 1962, the Musée National d'Art Moderne in Paris presented a vast exhibition of his work, covering collages, drawings, temperas, tapestries, fabrics, reliefs, assemblages, paintings, sculptures, lithographs, and *papiers déchirés*.

Arp has always let himself be guided by the individual circumstances of the moment, considering himself "integrated into the world"; however, in his definition of "concrete art," as opposed to the overvague "abstract," he has constantly affirmed: "We do not aim at copying nature, at 'reproducing,' but at producing directly, without need for an intermediary. Since there is not the slightest trace of abstraction in this work, we shall call it 'concrete art.' ... Concrete art is a natural, healthy, elemental art, which inspires the eternals of peace, love, and poetry in the mind and heart. When concrete art appears, despondency packs its gloomy thoughts in its dirty valises and withdraws."

Just as he had been a Dadaist (1916), Arp was also a Surrealist (1922–28), after close friendships from his youth onward with Max Ernst, Kandinsky (1912), and Mondrian (1926). In every act or event in his life, Arp has always gone beyond any rigid definition, leaving behind Dadaism, Surrealism, or concrete art, in the name of poetry faithfully served and followed through a creative process extraordinarily complex in its wealth of spiritual themes, the diversity of its sources, and the freedom of its artistic formation. "I take off like a bird," said Arp recently, "in a state of innocence and confidence. I never say 'I will now do this or that or the other.' I slowly approach the material and then take control of it. This is the most mysterious part, my hands work on their own, as if everything were happening a long way away from me and I were not necessary. The forms shape themselves: I simply watch. When I begin to like them I know they have become part of me." This is Arp's real spirit, smiling and romantic, a little ironic and with something of the dreamer, faithful to nature, and opposed to any form of rationality, with his astonishment undiminished each time he watches the birth and growth of a work dictated by the mysterious laws of the individual case.

"We are an integral part of the world: the forms we create with our hands depend inevitably on this: they pin down reality and make it more familiar."

Every idea (Arp has been described as the greatest inventor of forms of our century) has found an unprecedented material expression in reality; and while some of Arp's forms may have appeared as simple amusements or gratuitous experimentation by contrast with their times, they have all later, sometimes years later, shown themselves to be archetypes, molds for innumerable other forms. For example, the two painted wood reliefs, *Forest* and *Portrait of Tristan Tzara's Shadow, or Configuration* (1916); the wooden elements fixed to canvas, *Trousse d'un Da (Da-Set)* (1920); the collage *According to the Laws of Chance* (1916); the *Premier Papier Déchiré* (1932); the woven hanging *Cymétrie Pathétique* (1916–17); the painting *Crucifié* (1914); the relief *Constellation of Three White Forms on a Grey Ground* (1930) — the list could go on forever.

None of these works bore any resemblance to anything in existence at the time of their creation; there is no connection with Cubism or Futurism. Dada is the incarnation of a creative spirit without cultural intermediaries; Dada is the antithesis of any imitation, whether of an idiom or of an object.

In 1920 *Trousse d'un Da* must have been as incomprehensible as Schwitters' *Merz*; the *Premier Papier Déchiré* must have seemed a childish game in 1930, and the same was probably true of the wood constellations and the collages. As it was, this apparent escape from art really signified a profound participation in the objects created, liberating the sense of a primordial poetic reality: thus it was well ahead of the times in which these objects nevertheless took form. Arp rejects later interpretations of these archetypes of modern art. After more than forty years, he declares that certain present-day interpretations are completely useless, because Dada cannot be re-created in a totally different historical situation.

Perhaps this denial is too categorical, for the vitality of some of Arp's forms has been revealed precisely through later experiments and research, which cannot be considered only as formalistic, cultural essays. The revival of Dada seems to confirm its continued relevance, and thus, the universality of the forms that Arp created entirely on his own.

From 1930 onward, sculpture began to dominate Arp's activity. Over the past thirty years or so, his sculptural output has presented the most varied and rich formal repertory of our times, from the *Goblin's Head* of 1930 to the four granite *Forest Wheels* of 1961. The word "repertory" is accurate in this context, for concretions alternate with torsos, configurations with goblets, metamorphoses with wheels, with the result that there can be no precise formal categories. Naturally, each work has its own emphatic individuality. More generally, it can be said that Arp achieves the boldest syntheses without disowning even the most extreme polemics of Dada, without refusing the influences of prehistoric art, in a resumption of the relationship between man and the world which, as Carola Giedion-Welcker rightly points out, allows him to approach the "forces and laws of life" and make them his own.

The marble *Human Concretion* of 1934 is formed of a mass of volumes fused together in the representation of a healthy, sensual carnality. They correspond to the forces of concretion "which led to the concretion of the earth and the stars, of stones and plants and animals and men. Concretion is the product of growth." Another type of "concretion" is *Mounted on Oval Dish* (1948); here, the base is an integral part of the work, as in earlier object-sculptures such as *Bell and Navels* (1931), which bear a strong resemblance to Surrealist objects. Indeed, this had spurred Arp to write, "Certain Surrealist objects are at the same time concrete works. Stripped of all descriptive content, they strike me as being very important in the development of concrete art since, with their allusive means, they bring art the psychic emotions that give it life." The surreality of the image in another object-sculpture, *Getting Lost in the Woods* (1932), does not, however, obscure the Brancusi-inspired solution of the two bases incorporated into the sculpture — a difficult solution which prompted Arp to say, "The base...that's a long story."

Concretion, then, is the result of growth, and *Growth* was precisely the title Arp gave to a bronze dated 1938, in which the development of the forms takes on the organic character of a trunk or roots in a contorted verticality that reappears in some recent works, such as *Very Tall Person* (1960) and *Sculpture-Column* (1961). The serpentine movement of the "figures" recalls a visual impression that remained in

Figure 7 - Georges Vantongerloo (1886-): *Construction of Volumes*, plaster, 1918

Arp's memory after his frequent visits to the snake house in the zoo. The metamorphosis of *Cobra-Centaur* (1952) gives one some idea of the effect this impression had on his elaboration of images.

On the other hand, the series of *Torsos* from the 1931, 1938, and 1953 versions to the 1959 *Pyrenees Torso* tackles, as does the *Meudon Venus*, the problem of the organic vitalization of a traditional model reviewed in the present as a new discovery —which it was for the artist, especially after his stays in the south of France and Greece. Here we have a strange interpretation of Classical *stasis* set in the reality implied by Arp's rhythms: an interpretation that transforms everything in a sort of occult, dreamlike light.

The trunk, too, transforms itself into a giant torso, which Arp himself called *Spectral Moon-Man* because of the intense chiaroscuro out of which the work emerges like a phantom, as well as the energy of the plastic mass that was already to be seen in the 1938 "automatic sculpture" entitled *Homage to Rodin*. This is an unexpected tribute to the master of overtly sensual nudes: a more apt homage might have been the *Wreath of Breasts* of 1945 (Plate XLIII), which seems the unambiguous symbol of the sensual grace of certain Fontainebleau-school painters, reproduced in an allusive, three-dimensional reality.

The Classical idea dominates in the 1950 *Idol* (Plate XLV), the ironic representation of a mythological divinity made in the image of a metaphysical display manikin. The 1953 *Shepherd of the Clouds* (Plate XLIV) is a figure straight from an abstract poetic dream; it acquires its true dimension in terms of its setting, whether, as in 1954, beside the Yverdon Tower or, as now, at the University of Caracas. *Shepherd of the Clouds* is a synthesis of the most characteristic elements of Arp's art. Though inspired by contact with nature, its forms resemble nothing, reproduce nothing; they simply live as pure expressions of sentiment and spirit. No monumental sculpture by Arp exists in France: one dreams of seeing *Shepherd of the Clouds* installed in Paris rather than in Caracas.

Dream of the Owl (1947) is one of the purest images created by Arp in a state of cosmic faith and spiritual surrender. We have another metaphysical dream in the granite *Thales of Miletus* (1951), a truly superhuman, mysterious monument.

The "open" sculptures, *Ptolemy I* (1950) and *Ptolemy II* (1958), are unusual for Arp. Forms pierced with three openings, their rhythmic development supported by the hollowed-out armature, they are shot through with light in a space that dominates them. But Arp's true vitality consists in the dynamic vitality of the plastic organism, in the continual changes of outline that transform the full volumes in the supple mobility of the forms. On the other hand, the *Wheels* seem dictated by a desire to create closed forms, smooth on the circumferences and in the openings, rough on the flat surfaces. They are a homage to the mystic cults of prehistoric peoples, and perhaps a search for an elementary monumental idiom: the wheel, nothing but the wheel, with all its symbolic meaning. Before this, in 1943, Arp had applied the constellation theme to commemorate his wife Sophie Taeuber in *Construction of White Flowers in Memory of a Dead Woman* (Plate XLII). The cult of the dead and the wheel of time, in two unparalleled formal inventions, belong to the era's most poetic kingdom: Arcady.

The multiplicity of forms discovered by Arp, referring to the eternal themes of life and death, from germination through growth to concretion and concluding on a level of high dignity and stylistic purity, fulfills the artist's aspiration toward an art "that leads to spirituality and mystic reality." And, indeed, the former Dadaist joker, capable of all sorts of hoaxes and ironic humor to irritate the bourgeoisie of his youth, reveals himself as a completely pure poet who, through his art, wants "to transform the world, to make existence more bearable, to save man from his most dangerous folly — vanity; to simplify man's life, to identify it with nature, for reasoning wrenches man out of his original setting and forces him into a life of tragedy." Arp longs to save man by the example of his life as a poet. And his life as a poet is indissolubly linked to his poems and sculptures, that is, with dreams beyond reality, beyond reason, "according to the laws of chance."

Reason, on the other hand, was the slogan and battle cry for the work of Antoine Pevsner (1884—1962), born in Orel and naturalized French in 1930. When he arrived in Paris in 1911, Pevsner, who already knew the most important avant-garde painting, fully represented in Russia in the Morozov and Tzukin collections, admired above all the Eiffel Tower, which struck him as a memorable example of Constructivist sculpture.

Pevsner and his brother Naum Gabo, in the *Realistic Manifesto*, which was written in Moscow, published by the state presses, and posted in all the streets of the city, declared their aim of abolishing the solid mass that did not express space and replacing it with emptiness. The work was to be constructed, hence the term "constructivism: a movement based on the philosophy of space and time."

Art had to be pure, uncontaminated by any figurative element; and in order to correspond to reality, it had to be based on space and time. Volume is not the only concept of space. Kinetic and dynamic elements must be used to express the true nature of time: static rhythms are not enough. The volumes of mass and space are not, in plastic terms, the same thing; they are two distinct, concrete, measurable materials. Space must become an integral part of the work. Art must no longer be imitative: it must discover new forms.

Similar ideas are to be found more than once in the canons of various avant-garde artists. But none had succeeded in theorizing with the rational rigor of Pevsner and Gabo who, with the rise to political supremacy of Stalin, were to be classed with Kandinsky and Malevich as "purveyors of art to decadent capitalists." The two brothers were thus forced to seek a more congenial climate in which to "purvey" their work, and demonstrate the truth of their prodigiously advanced conceptions. In 1926, with the celluloid and zinc *Portrait of Marcel Duchamp*, Pevsner, using light, transparent plastics, had already begun to see *inside* the sculpture and destroy its smooth, impenetrable outer surface. For the first time "light and shadow penetrated into the very heart of the sculpture, which soaked them up like a sponge."

The steps from conception to realization, from transparent to open forms, are marked by a succession of works, including *Extensible Surfaces* and *Projections in Space* (1938—39), *Fresco* (1944), *Extensible Chain of Victory* (1945—46), *Universe* (1947), *Embryonic Construction* (1948; Plate XLVIII), *Dynamic Projection at 30°* (1950—51), *Peace Column* (1954), *Liberation of the Spirit* (1955—56), and *Spectral Vision* (1959).

In order to arrive at the expression of that depth which is "the only form of expression for space" and the dynamic rhythms that replaced "the static rhythms which for millennia the Egyptians considered the only element of art," Pevsner had to choose, in the course of countless experiments, the materials suited to his conceptions and new techniques — materials capable of expressing fully the new reality, which has too often been equated with a scientific reality, a mere mathematical formula.

"Drawing" the sculpture in space was accomplished with wires soldered together; and the various extensible surfaces were suggested by lattices of aluminum or other metal wires. The actual construction demanded long periods of work, sometimes an entire year, before the sculpture reached its definitive form. Pevsner was convinced that the new conceptions and forms would open the door to another world, until then little explored. Over and above this, he and Gabo had aimed at achieving "a synthesis of the arts: painting, sculpture, and architecture."

Contrary to all expectations, Pevsner's pure art has found practical uses in Detroit and Caracas, thanks to the architects Saarinen and Villanueva. It has taken its place in everyday life as an element of poetic suggestion, not merely as an ornamental adjunct of architecture.

His extensible constructions composed "in accordance with a flight toward the interior" reproduce in reverse a process of creation and generation. Space and time are reconciled in the dynamic rhythm assumed by the surfaces in their development, governed by an abstract formal logic. Pevsner's lucid intelligence was always turned toward the absolute of stylistic perfection, as if to a supreme aesthetic and ethical end. In fact, Pevsner himself declared that the work of art "must spread harmony and peace" among the fatigue and insecurity of modern men, rather than disturb them further with monstrous symbols of horror and anguish.

With perfect coherency Pevsner sustained in every one of his works what Herbert Read calls "the absolute clarity of a Euclidean theorem." This absolute clarity is the mainspring of his art, as opposed to the irrationality prevalent in more immediately contemporary work. As things are, Pevsner is remembered in an ideologically hostile present mainly for his definite historical contribution to the most extreme current of international purism.

With Alberto Giacometti (1901–) and Max Ernst, another current of modern sculpture takes shape: Surrealism. Giacometti took his first steps in sculpture in the studio of Bourdelle, who obliged him to copy figures from life. But Giacometti never quite managed to copy them, for his vision changed every day: the model gave him endless problems, for at the time he found representation impossible. In a recent interview, Giacometti said that it was this feeling of impossibility that led him to abandon reality and present it only from memory. "For ten years [from 1925 on] I created exclusively from memory, beyond the limits of truth. Until 1935 I tried all possible methods. Even abstraction."

His flight from reality had begun with *Two People* (1926), which was an intelligent, slightly ironic tribute to Negro sculpture; then with *Spoon Woman* (1927) he moved toward the construction of objects, the miraculous open boxes and airy cages of *Suspended Sphere* (1930) and *The Palace at Four in the Morning* (1932–33), among the sculptor's most surreal inventions, and in 1934 he conceived the *Head* which is built up on a framework of abstract, geometrical architecture. Giacometti is the one sculptor who has managed to translate the "dreams" of his imagination into artistically valid images. His fantastic constructions, set in the irrational domain of the arbitrary, establish a new relationship between object and space. In *The Palace at Four in the Morning* the metaphysical representation of space leaves a disconcerting sense of emptiness and cosmic solitude, while *Suspended Sphere* blends geometry and surreality in an absurd play on effects. During this period (1925–35), Giacometti dragged up from the depths of his memory, which had been profoundly influenced by modern cultural influences, magical idols and fetishes, bizarre, obsessional images, sadistic amusements, and ironic parodies.

His disgust with reality stemmed from the fact that he found it impossible to see the figure as a whole: only details were retained in his vision. In *The Palace at Four in the Morning*, as in *Suspended Sphere*, the slim bars outline the cage box in terms of graphically conceived lines. They are thus representations of a whole, set in a tangible perspective — all that Giacometti had vainly tried to achieve in perspective synthesis of the human figure.

But Giacometti's Surrealist period was only a parenthesis inspired not merely by disgust with reality, but also by human and intellectual sympathy with the group of artists who, with rare intelligence and a civilized sense of irony, had undertaken to follow the way of Surrealism. The parenthesis lasted ten years, and was only halted in 1935 by the artist's decision to return to the model, to copy a head. And indeed, every day from 1935 to 1940, Giacometti set himself to copy a head, never succeeding but still obstinately, determinedly starting afresh the next day. Art for Giacometti is a means toward an end, and the end is *seeing*. A difficult means, since for five long years that one head was to escape him more every day, elusive as a will-o'-the-wisp; but the artist did not let negative results discourage him from his Herculean task. As Giacometti himself said, "Such activity is completely useless to society. Extremely self-centered and inconvenient, really. Yet it's the immediate sensation of the present that you feel when you try to pin down reality. The greatest adventure is seeing something new in the same face every day — better than a trip round the world." The adventure begins when one resumes contact with reality.

"As far as I am concerned," continues Giacometti, "the greatest invention is one and the same thing as the greatest resemblance." One copies the vision that remains in each instant, that is, the image that becomes conscious. "Modern sculptors aim at capturing their sensation of reality rather than reality itself. In any case it would be impossible to capture every aspect. What can be possessed is only the appearance: all that is left is the reality of the appearance. If a person is standing five feet away, or fifty, I cannot draw him back into the truth of positive reality. If I am sitting on a café terrace and people walk past on the opposite sidewalk, I see them tiny. Their real dimensions no longer exist."

And indeed, Giacometti's tenacity was so great that in five years, and from 1940 to the present day, the screen that kept him from seizing the character of a face or calculating the true dimensions of a body gradually fell away.

During his Surrealist period, Giacometti had made fantastic sculpture-objects, relying on his memory, which suggested primitive art and elements from archaeology to be incorporated into a modern expressive idiom. A figurative sculpture must start from a detail, like an eye, then complete itself in every element until it becomes a head or a nude, almost by spontaneous generation. Behind the theories and observations with which Giacometti seeks to justify the thickness of a face or the vertical elongation and slenderness of his figures — the sculptor claims to have been inspired by the mobile, darting figurines of Callot — this memory is always present.

The basic framework of the sculpture is reduced virtually to a single wire, covered with a little clay or plaster. Hieratic idols rise side by side on their cubic bases — the bases, too, are integral parts of the works — and stand like votive statuettes in their pure, spiritual grace and elegance. For many long years, Giacometti tried to give form to a vision turned once more toward truth; and truth is always a kind of surreal transfiguration. "Sculpture is supported by the void. Space is hollowed out to construct the object and the object in its turn creates space."

To compose his visual material in a unified image that "creates space," Giacometti has always followed an absolutely intuitive method of juxtaposition and separation, based on empirical observation, which nevertheless permits him to express his theories on visibility in poetic terms. Photographs have shown that the relationship between the larger vertical figures and their environment, when they are placed on a Parisian sidewalk, is correct, and the same is true of comparison with the open hand, which then seems a votive offering. The figurines' perspective in space corresponds to the angle of a distorting point of view — which for Giacometti is truth. Seen from above and set at a distance, the figures lose all distinctive characteristics, they are simply outlines reduced to the minute dimensions of prehistoric Sardinian nuraghic bronzes arranged on a plane surface that corresponds to their spatial environment. Giacometti claims to have based this on observations made in Venice. Indeed, *The Piazza* of 1948–49 (Plate L) gives precisely this impression of distance, in which man loses his individuality and becomes an indistinct blur. (Morally, too, this is always one way of seeing things.) The busts have greater consistency because of their frontality, which contrasts with the sharp profiles of faces individualized in all their human variety, as the result of a slow process of formal investigation. These busts are foreshadowed in the drawings and virtually monochrome paintings that Giacometti still executes in the semi-darkness of his studio, hollowing out the canvas, one might almost say, for he is deeply preoccupied with relief and environment.

Just as Medardo Rosso modeled with wax, Giacometti works with successive additions of clay and so obtains chiaroscuro effects on his active, highly contrasted surfaces. His walking figures, those strange, bald creatures poised on stilts, and the female nudes that are turned into beanpoles by the verticality of their gesture and pose (like the famous Etruscan nude in the Volterra Museum) inspired Germaine Richier's monsters. Though turning his back on official Surrealism, Giacometti has created the archetype of a new expressive figuration: through tireless research he has summoned the ghosts of the invisible out of the faraway realm of dream and incubus, always convinced that the reality of the vision is leading him closer to the profound human reality of the image. With his exceptionally acute observation of reality, Giacometti has been the master of a whole generation of modern artists by virtue of the curious contradiction shown in the great vitality of his sculpture.

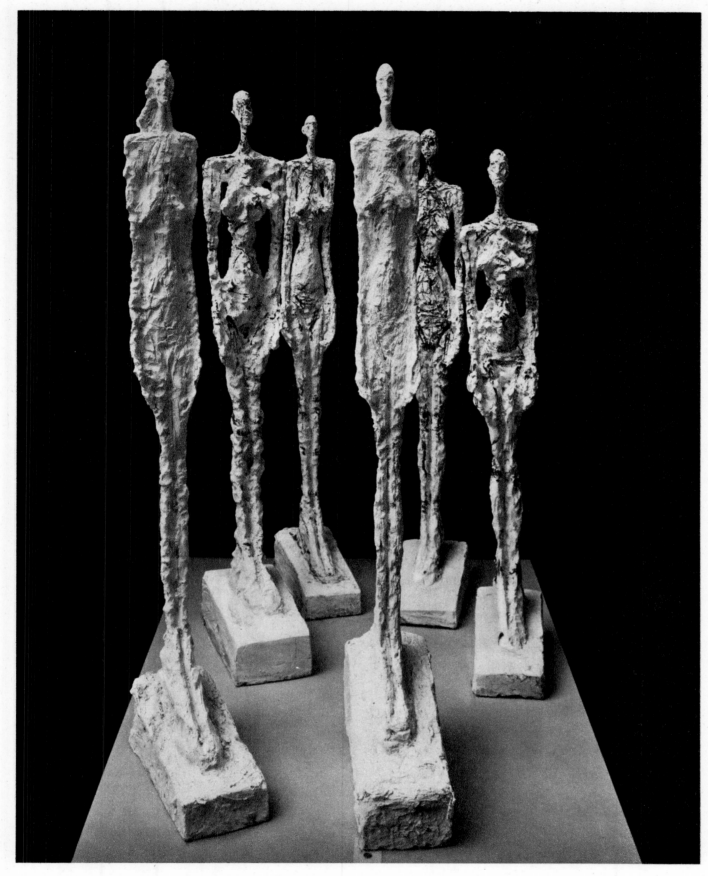

Figure 8 - Alberto Giacometti (1901-): *Six Figures*, plaster, 1955-56.

In his youth in Venice, Giacometti was possessed by admiration for Tintoretto, for the élan of the old master's elongated figures catapulted into space, and he has often returned to Venice, the city best suited to his meditation and observations on art and reality.

The tension of forms in a work such as *Six Figures* of 1955–56 (figure 8) expresses the artist's spiritual tension, stemming from the will to know, which, with a profound moral commitment, is the prerequisite demanded by art as a means for reaching truth.

By rights, Giacometti belongs to a history devoted only to those protagonists destined to remain as the interpreters of the civilization of our age. He is indeed one of the protagonists, even when he sees fit to go against the current of his times: a tormented, worried personality around whom a veritable romantic legend has grown up. But his anguish is resolved in his extraordinary figures and not in snippets of biography. He is the exact opposite of Arp, Brancusi, and Pevsner, the antithesis of programmatic purism: he follows the stylistic formula of pagan idols, which stand out against all modern sculpture in their disconcerting truthfulness. With his constantly reformulated theories of vision in terms of space, and the sculptures that demonstrate these theories in the most poetic way imaginable, Giacometti the sculptor occupies a place in the front rank of the history of modern art.

While Giacometti's Surrealist period was limited to only ten years, Max Ernst (1891–) has continued the Surrealist experiment, showing immense imaginative resources in the various techniques he uses in painting, sculpture, graphic work, and collage, all reflecting his taste for the extravagant indulged through a macabre sense of humor, intellectual gratuitousness, and acrobatics of irony. Max Ernst is one of those artists who cannot be imagined outside the setting of a particular culture, which becomes the mainspring of their creative activity.

Following the example set by Marcel Duchamp, Ernst amused himself looking for the strangest analogies in *objets trouvés* — that is, in everyday objects on which the artist bestows aesthetic value by means of an arbitrary, polemical decision. His search for these objects led him to discover new materials, to be used in sculpture to achieve particular suggestive effects. Dadaist objects which, as we have seen, were made up of heterogeneous elements (pieces of wood, wire, bits of metal, rope, parts of machinery) and were originally intended simply to provoke the onlooker, later revealed unsuspected expressive possibilities. The current reappraisal of the Dada phenomenon is not due to the caprice of a sterile, bored society; on the contrary, it is truly a discovery, in critical and poetic terms, of the works of a given historical moment, which up till now had been considered purely polemical.

In 1927 it seemed very eccentric to exhibit, instead of a sculpture, an ordinary pebble. Max Ernst did just this, to ridicule a certain part of society. Then in 1934 he began to be obsessed by sculpture, during a visit to Giacometti's house in Maloia, when the capricious Italian was in the process of abandoning surreality for reality. Ernst would go out and hunt in the streams for pebbles polished by the water; he then scratched their surfaces, but without changing their over-all form, for he claimed that he was only completing what nature had begun. The engraved granite took on the appearance of primitive fragments, of simulated archaeological specimens.

Ernst's sculptures are always marked by magical or ritual cultures, and so acquire esoteric, rather ambiguous significance, from the two versions of *Oedipus* (1934) to *Moon-asparagus* (1935) and *King Playing with Queen* of 1954 (Plate LII). Cultural influences are never lacking in his work, and there are continual allusions to symbols borrowed from extra-European mythologies and religions. His penchant for the unknown and the rare is applied with subtle intelligence to make masks and idols: *Mother and Daughter* (1959), *Spirit of the Bastille* (1960), *Beautiful Souls* (1961). Ernst has always remained faithful to his earliest Dadaist initiation, in Cologne in 1919, and to Surrealist symbolism.

The recent masks could be a real anthology of pre-Columbian art, from Mexico to Peru, in interpretations of ironic parody or oneiric poetry. They range over the world of dreams and the strangest metamorphoses, for Ernst's imagination is turned to the darkest corners of human psychology, ancient religions, secret rituals. Surprises are plentiful, for Ernst is a past master in the art of drawing unexpected images out of the world of dreams and making them acceptable as facts, albeit fantastic, of daily reality, marvelous discoveries in normal, day-to-day existence, often changing the order and logical meaning of words and objects. According to the man himself, "Sculpture is made in an embrace, with two hands, as one makes love. It is the most simple art, and the most primitive. I never have to force or guide myself. Sculpture does not need the concentration or effort that painting demands." Ernst turns his sculptures into fabulous, fantastic characters: his imagination is anthropomorphic, so as to give body to the figures of the unknown, the figures that live and hide in images that contradict the times, in a reality that consists entirely of culture, however rarefied or exotic.

Henri-Georges Adam (1904–) set himself the problem of integrating the various arts. Attempted solutions are to be found, where architecture and sculpture are concerned, in *Habitable Architecture-Sculpture* (1951), which was entered in the International Contest for a Monument to the Unknown Political Prisoner, and *Habitable Architecture-Sculpture (Pharos)* (1954); and in the case of engraving and sculpture, *Engraved Woman* (1949), which inaugurates the series of sculptures culminating in *Marine Mutations* (1956–60) and *Cryptograms* (1961). Adam then set the same problem to his pupils in the École Nationale des Beaux-Arts; working in groups, they collaborated to produce several large habitable sculptures that were shown in the 1961 Paris Biennale. Adam has drawn inspiration from Le Corbusier and the Ronchamp chapel, but he never fails to impose his personality as a sculptor. The son of a jeweler, Adam practiced the goldsmith's art in his early youth, before devoting himself to the patient task of engraving, in which his exceptional sense of contrast has placed him among the foremost masters of this century. He then turned his attention to larger things, to grandiose monumental projects.

Working on a large scale does not rule out the danger of a certain grandiloquence, but for Adam "working big" implies obedience to a true vocation, and a very precise conception of monumental sculpture. His feeling for size is directly related to his feeling for nature, which gives him some of his broadest, most inspired visions. A perfect unity of style closely links his sculptures to the big black-and-white tapestries and the large engravings.

Some time spent on the coast of Brittany brought Adam back to the sea, the poetry of the ocean and natural elements. This marine spirit animates the great New York and Le Havre tapestries, and the engravings *Stones, Sand, and Water* (1956–57), *The Long Earth* (1957), *Watchtower* and *Wrecks* (1959), and *Earth* (1960). When, in 1948, Adam began to sculpt the *Large Nude* in the great hall of Boisgeloup — the work was shown in the Galérie Maeght in 1949 — the basic idea, still closely related to nature, was dominated by the monumentality of the forms. The great plaster was articulated on the supporting plane surfaces in an alternation of abstract and realistic outlines, with an elemental cohesive force that, with the unity of its style, gave the work the appearance of nature itself. Force of nature, force of the earth expressed in a measure at once abstract and sensual, this great sculpture which stemmed from the 1945 Laurens-inspired *Sleeping Woman* opened the way through its structural conception toward architecture-sculpture. Six years later, the conception was to be translated into reality, first in the sycamore-wood sketch for the Le Havre monument, then in cement in the monument itself, which stretches over seventy feet in front of the new museum, facing the harbor mouth (Plate LIV).

The sketch conveys exactly the movement of the sharp, geometrical form, which seems to lunge forward in space. The enormous dimensions of the work presented considerable static and constructional problems, all of which were foreseen and resolved by the sculptor himself. Today the finished monument is installed on its base in dynamic equilibrium: the tension of its forms suggests a leap or flight toward the immensity of the ocean and the sky. Thus the dream of Adam, who had already conceived *Pharos for the Dead* (1957–58: not executed) for the Auschwitz monument, has been realized in Le Havre, in the maritime environment dear to the sculptor's heart, and in harmony with the character and atmosphere of the city.

Pharos for the Dead, too, is simultaneously architecture and sculpture in the square-set bareness of its forms and the geometrical structure that is found in all Adam's works, even in his most expressionist sculpture, such as the *Tomb-figure* (1943). The latter, when shown in 1944 at the Salon de la Libération, scandalized the public but met with Picasso's admiring approval. Before Adam's meeting with Picasso, there is in his sculpture a certain suggestion of Surrealism, shown at its most interesting in the sculptures, masks, and figurines (1942) for Sartre's *The Flies*, produced by Dullin in the Théâtre de la Cité in July 1943.

His Surrealist development took place outside the movement itself, and so was completely independent of the aesthetic theories and passion for experiment of Dali, Masson, and Ernst. His illustrations for Gérard de Nerval's *Les Chimères* are lucid, marvelous enchantments pinned down in exact, implacable signs in an atmosphere of pure surreality. Adam's imagination, freely unleashed on Nerval's metaphysical texts, becomes identified with the poetic symbols of the seasons, the sea, sky, beaches, and forests. His overriding feeling for nature suggested *Boats* of 1956, *The Wave* of 1959 (Plate LV), *Ship's Wheel* of 1959, *Nautilus* of 1959, *Saint Matthew's Point* of 1960, *Three Points* of 1960 from the Marine Mutations cycle, and the four Cryptograms of 1961: *Mask, Flower, Arrow,* and *Leaf*. In these sculptures, the smooth surfaces bear magical engraved and drawn signs, which contrast with the lines of the pure geometrical forms. The incorporation of these graphic elements is typical of Adam. As early as *Engraved Woman* (1949) the graphic signs were enclosed in rectangular spaces reminiscent of paneling, but ill-adapted to the character of the sculpture, whose over-all form seemed to hesitate between the cover of a mummy case and a money box. In recent works the relief drawing gives a rare, precious quality to the image, completing it and suggesting comparison with ideograms of ancient civilizations. *Horned Beast* (1947) is related to Picasso's artistic fauna. *Three Points* (1960) is a curious interpretation of exotic plants, marked with an arabesque of parallel horizontal bands in relief, seen before in *The Wave*, which give the sculptures precious ornamental richness.

The process of abstraction leads to pure forms, which Adam uses on the large scale in his habitable architecture-sculptures. His teachings at the Beaux-Arts emphasize the moral value of collective collaboration in works that are intended to repeat the miracle of the building of the Romanesque cathedrals. Beside his larger undertakings, Adam still executes objects carved or engraved with the minute manual care of a goldsmith. In short, with the simplicity of his origins, which he has never once betrayed in the course of a career rich in experience, he embodies a complex artistic development which, by virtue of the vastness of the man's conceptions and the serious study he devotes to them, strikes one as having an almost Renaissance feeling and character.

Émile Gilioli (1911–) aims at the absolute, crystallized in the conceptual unity of forms positioned and declared in space. Geometry is allied with imagination in a marriage free from contradictions, for it results in the exact dimension of the plastic mass. While he does not really resemble Pevsner, Gilioli does tend toward pure form and prefers the most durable materials. In an age of ironwork, when the final result often depends on chance, Gilioli concentrates on good workmanship, like the perfect craftsman he is.

"When I make a sculpture," says Gilioli, "I feel that I am completely myself and sometimes succeed in finding my own reality." Thus the sculptor rediscovers the old joy when as a child he amused himself "carving pears, heavy and live in the hand."

In his youth, Gilioli worked as a blacksmith, a maker of "useful" objects in which he discerned an elementary formal beauty, a primordial harmony. But his closeness to personalities like Brancusi, Arp, and Laurens was a determining influence for Gilioli, who remained in the atmosphere, natural for him, of stylistic purism. His forms are crystalline, sharply angled, except in *Isolina* of 1949–56 (Plate LVII), and finished like *objets d'art*: *Little Sphere* (1947), *Eternal Dwelling* (1958) in bronze, *Sea and Sky* (1955), and the Baccarat crystal *Imprisoned Bird* (1958). Alongside the small sculptures, which reflect their spatial environment as if in a many-faceted mirror and so participate in their setting, Gilioli works from other principles to create the great geometrical masses of his monumental sculptures, solemn and absolute, like menhirs or steles.

The marble *Waiting* (1957), the Carrara *Caterpillar* (1957), and the sketch for the Unknown Political Prisoner could become majestic monuments. These sculptures are conceived in terms of marble; they have the weight and solemnity of marble in their positioning and their elementary geometrical structure. Gilioli conceives his forms in monumental terms, which are best suited for representing a synthesis of art, nature, and life. Indeed, his large sculptures enter into reality and define it.

Gilioli's purism is colored with humane feeling, far removed from the rigid intransigence of certain programmatic artists. The secret of the vitality of his forms stems from his ability to look at and love, with the same enthusiasm, a pebble from a stream, a beautiful woman, a tree, a pre-Columbian carving, a flower, or a Romanesque chapel. Gilioli arrives at his severity of style by a very human participation in things, rather than pure cerebral calculation, and so escapes the dangers of academic purism.

"The essential virtues of the work of Morice Lipsi (1898–) are precisely his purity and truth," says Gindertael concluding a selection of the sculptor's work. And indeed, purity and truth are expressed in the blocks of marble, stone, or lava or in the wood-carvings, sculpted with a desire for the absolute. Heart, torso, trunk, milestone, and circle become significant forms in Lipsi's art, rediscovered structures shown in their simple, elemental architecture (Plates LVIII–LIX).

The dark lava *Heart* is one of these forms: a block whose porous surface seems to express by the very nature of the material a sense of timeless antiquity and belonging to nature. It is a symbolic form intended, one might think, as an imaginary offering to the generous gods of poetry. Through the metamorphoses of art, milestones are transformed into signposts marking the passage of time, primordial images of an invented history, menhirs raised to the sky but still tied to the earth by the weight of their material. Milestones, stones corroded by time into the forms of pedestals or rough anvils, are no longer useful objects necessary for the life of primitive man: they are images of the return to first sources, which is the pilgrimage made by our modern civilization in search of a natural way of living and working.

Lipsi erected a monumental sculpture in local stone on the road to Bordeaux; it immediately became part of the landscape, in a dimension harmonizing with the plain, the trees, and the far-off hills. He knows all the techniques of the ancients and always works with an eye to durability in the silence and solitude of his retreat at Chevilly-la-Rue. Purity and truth are more than mere words when applied to his work.

Étienne Hajdu (1907–) was trained in Bourdelle's studio, admired Rodin, but finally opted for Romanesque and, after traveling in Greece and Crete, post-Phidian Grecian art. It may be that Hajdu does not share Maillol's hatred for Praxiteles. Certainly Praxiteles, too, worked marble with the same soft, sensitive elegance shown by Hajdu, who spent the second World War working in a marble quarry in the Pyrenees: useful experience. As we have so often seen, every artist has experience as an artisan; however, Hajdu does not limit himself to marble. Every material is good for the artist who knows what he wants to do, without depending on the block of stone or the tree trunk for inspiration. Hajdu has declared squarely that "where the material ends, art begins," contrary to many present-day experiments where there is a tendency to take the various materials as motives for creation.

At the summit of his maturity, for his exhibit at the Galérie Jeanne Bucher in 1961, Hajdu grouped a series of figures in black and white Greek marble, polished with incorporeal softness where different planes meet. His sculptures are physically shallow, made to be viewed frontally in the beauty of their outlines, which are affirmed in a dimension of ideal purity. This inspired Dora Vallier to say, "As if by a miracle so indispensable one hardly dares believe in its existence, Hajdu has made sculpture that overcomes contradictions and reveals an immediate purity and a new form

48

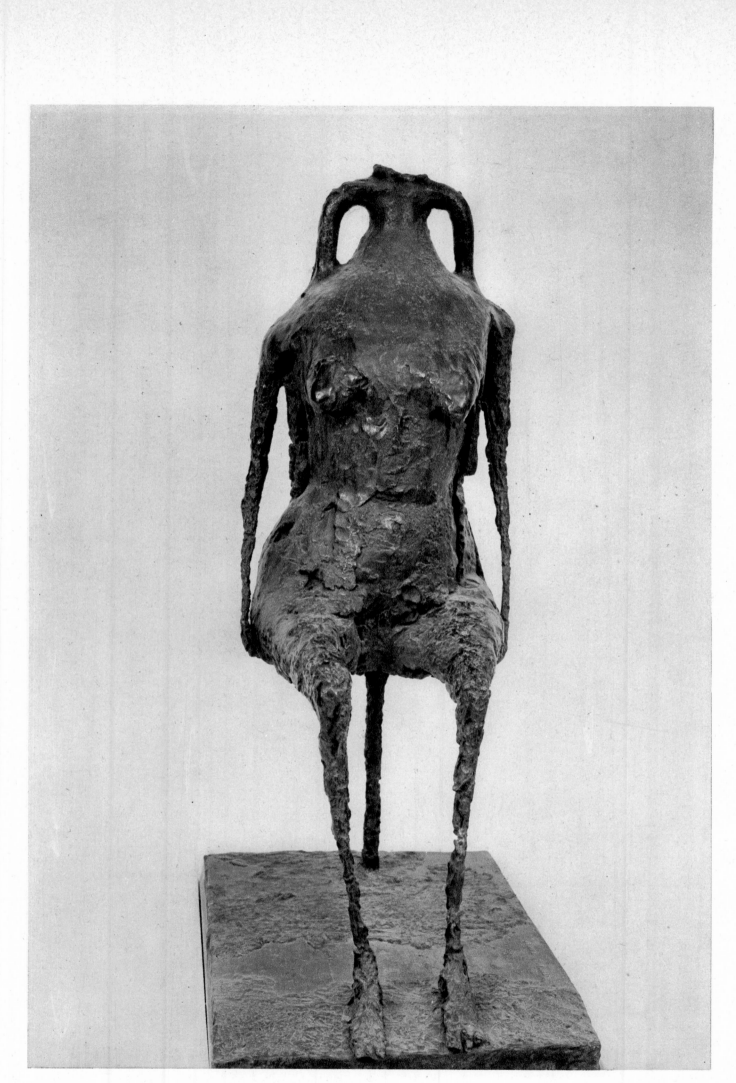

Figure 9 - Germaine Richier (1904-1959): *Water*, bronze, 1953-54.

which, like our perception of reality, is constructed in a mobile space: the space we know today, but open wide to the light, as if it were stretching out toward a zenith." Light, in fact, is the true reward of Hajdu's sculptures, which in some cases reach the stylistic purity of the Cycladic idols they recall. His is a sculpture of supreme harmony and rare formal perfection.

Head (1960) and *Luba* (1961), both in Paro marble, *The Girls of My Town* of 1961 (Plate LX) and *Sylvia* of 1961, both in Pentelic marble, and *Veronica* (1960) in black marble, are "portraits" created out of Hajdu's abstract imagination; enigmatic, or rather, secret portraits that reveal an ideal conception of forms in the domain of a new, pure aesthetic that can no longer be compared with that of Brancusi or Arp.

Then there are the reliefs in copper, in lead, in beaten tin, rumpled and swelling, sometimes incorporating objects and pieces of machinery, the new decorative motifs that so many modern sculptors are trying to introduce into our living rooms; these alternate with sculptures in marble. *Offering to Gislebertus* (1960), derived from a beaten aluminum low relief, was cast in cement and set into the wall of a house.

Hajdu takes care to fit his unreal reliefs into the reality of modern life, at the same time stressing the nobility of their origins in the archaic motifs of Knossos. There is no contradiction in this, for contemporary civilization is reliving in the present every experience in the history of art. And in his search for a direction for his own sculptures, Hajdu ranges himself with the other artists who are fighting for an integration of the plastic arts.

André Bloc (1896–) is one of these. Bloc first devoted himself to sculpture in 1940, after having worked as an engineer, founding the review *L'Architecture d'Aujourd'hui* and proclaiming in innumerable essays and articles the necessity for an integration of the visual arts. Influenced at first by Brancusi and Arp and fired with an insatiable need for activity and a curiosity reawakened by every event or idea in contemporary art and philosophy, Bloc is incapable of shutting himself up in any set formula, and has tried his hand at every type and genre of sculpture, from Constructivism to the abstract. In this frenzied activity as a creator, planner, and organizer (in 1951 he founded the group Espace) he has always given the best of himself, placing particular stress on the importance of collective work, as in Teheran and Caracas. Dorfles, presenting Bloc in an exhibition in 1960, says, "An innate sense of the relationship of dimensions between buildings or natural environments and the work of art itself, enables him to study and elaborate the appropriate scale on which the work must be executed for the relationships to be coherent and harmonious."

Bloc is an organizer and a spreader of ideas: one of the modern spirits who have best grasped the lesson of the Renaissance. His artistic eclecticism does not permit him to fix himself to a single line of research. Every material and every form of plastic expression have been tried out in his hallucinating series of constructions open to space, which represent the infinite possibilities of the human imagination, from the "drawing" of interwoven wires to the works composed of fragments of metal soldered together to produce a mineralogical appearance.

André Bloc occupies a place apart in modern French sculpture; he cannot be classified in any particular category, because of his uncommitted, independent attitude toward the artistic phenomena of his time which he studies, exhausts, and

Figure 10 - Henri-Georges Adam (1904-): *Reclining Nude*, plaster, 1947-48.

improves on in the course of impassioned searching and lucid meditation of the aesthetic problems closely connected with these phenomena.

The personalities studied so far represent the currents in modern French sculpture that were stated and defined before the second World War and have continued their development or consolidation — both in the works dealt with up to this point and in the years to come.

In France, as in the rest of the world, the postwar period saw the rise of a whole new generation of artists who cannot be said to be without origins, insofar as they are related above all to the work of Picasso and Giacometti, but who propose in their completely different cultural environment a conception of sculpture far removed from any of the tenets of Purism or Constructivism. The period is marked by a resurgence of Expressionism through the channels opened by the most extreme Surrealist experiments. Surrealism had laid bare the world of the subconscious and the unconscious, often under the pretext of following a scientific method. It threw light on man's primordial fears and terrors, his obsessions and complexes, almost always in sexual terms. The desire for permanence, implicit in the work of a Brancusi, an Arp, or a Pevsner, is supplanted by uncertainty and distrust of time: by a sort of desperation, tacit or shouted loud, by the decadence of every faith, of every moral principle. The anguish of living in the present moment, the anxiety to miss nothing that life can afford in the way of pleasure, leads ultimately to boredom, dissatisfac-

51

tion, and *angst*. This lies at the heart of the decisive turn taken by contemporary civilization and culture.

In the specific field of sculpture, other elements contributed to its transformation that now, nineteen years after the end of the war, can be measured in its full breadth and depth and complexity. Some artists heralded the transformation in works expressing the incubus of recent suffering and a dark future in which, without exaggeration, the destruction of all humanity is perfectly possible.

Germaine Richier initiated the era of monsters; Étienne Martin and Stahly inaugurated the flight into nature: abnormal, mysterious, germinating, rich in overflowing forces and overloaded with sexual symbols and undertones.

Germaine Richier (1904—1959) outstepped the limits of traditional figuration in 1946 with her *Spider* and created the type of insect which, according to the prophets of science fiction, was to become master of the world when man has finished destroying himself. This was the malevolent insect, repeated in endless interpretations in modern sculpture, the dominant figure in a new bestiary that could perhaps be inspired by the same fear and anguish that stalked the nights of the Middle Ages.

Different historical conditions saw the repetition of the same phenomena, whether through the ignorance and collective brutalization of men — in the days when culture was for the exceptional few — or because of the excess of material goods offered by technological and scientific progress — when culture has become generalized in spite of the existence of men who still live in Stone-Age conditions. Germaine Richier intuitively felt this human situation right from the beginning, and represented it in comparison with natural forces in a few of her figures: *Storm* of 1947—48 (Plates LXII—LXIII), *Hurricane* of 1949, *Ogre* of 1951, and *The Spring* of 1953—54.

It has been suggested that Richier's fantastic world contains influences of Bosch, Ernst, and Ensor, but these influences are indirect, insofar as the world is inhuman and dramatic, constantly dominated by a sense of impending death. The repugnantly deformed, stick-like skeleton shows through in every figure. And when man himself becomes the symbol of antinatural forces he assumes the terrifying aspect of primitive man with his love for the horrible.

Richier's figures dominate space with the brooding presence of fantasy pushed to the extreme: an extreme space, too, tending toward the diabolical in its medieval plunging depth. Their fleshless emaciation descends from the thin style of Giacometti, but is dictated by another problem. As has been seen, Giacometti places modern figures in a perspective that sets them at a distance in time and space, so that he returns ultimately to Etruscan and Nuraghic idols. Germaine Richier is not concerned with style, but aims at expressive force and nothing else — thereby achieving true style.

In the *Storm* torso this force is modeled on the same plastic energy that animates the torso of Rodin's *Walking Man*. There is something absurd and bestial in the stocky figure; it seems born of the deepest strata of the earth, and dragged down by its own weight. Other figures, however, are suspended in mid-air, linked to wires that multiply them in space. The wires of *Spider's Web*, *Warriors*, *Ant*, *Devil*, and *Mandolin* are graphic elements inserted into sculpture to become tangled skeins or even the nucleus of a new sculptural representation, different from the threads in certain sculptures of Moore and the archetypal works, too often forgotten, of Giacomo Balla. The tangle of

Mandolin is woven in accordance with an organic process of formation. This has served as a point of departure for development, progressively more detached from the original nucleus, for many modern sculptors up to Claire Falkenstein.

Bourdelle's teaching, "learning to see," has been carried to its extreme consequences here — that is, to the point of penetrating into the very heart of nature and extracting its most mysterious elements. Later, Richier imposed a background on her isolated figures (a procedure sometimes employed in painting by artists like Hartung and Vieira da Silva) to establish precise spatial relationships. This is usually a sort of wall, straight or curved, which creates a clearly limited envinronment for the skeletal creatures or the malign, cruel little monsters the sculptress evoked from prehistory.

"Seeing inside" things, for Richier, implied discovering only their cruel and horrible side, translating them into the material reality of painted plaster, wires, lead, metals, and glass insets. Work was a long experiment, continually new and valid, a means of searching for a personal truth, up to the *Palms*, the little bronzes reminiscent of leaves and monstrances, and the characters of *Chessboard*. Germaine Richier's truth resides in the things revealed, midway between mystery and anguish, the disquieting muses of her imagination, in things defined in their most arid, desperate essence; in the surreal world of gigantic insects and thunderstruck zombies, which have been adopted as stylistic models by a horde of artists incapable of living, as Richier did, the drama of so tormented an existence.

She herself said, "I like tense, sinewy, dry things, olive trees dried up by the wind, brittle wood. . . . I am more moved by a charred tree stump than by an apple tree in flower." The sun of Van Gogh's Provençal madness, the sun of the Hérault on the Mediterranean, where the cicadas are masters of the land, has burned up all living forms and reduced them to skeletons. Germaine Richier has created the world of the mantis, so that even men end by resembling insects.

Another southerner, César (César Baldaccini) (1921—), obviously shares Richier's belief in the ghosts and hallucinations that spring from the sun and take on the same forms as the figures in Nordic fables, born in the darkness of forests, in snow and mist. César is a sculptor who works in iron, the extraordinary inventor of assemblages of *objets trouvés*, innumerable pieces of scrap metal welded together to replace the costly traditional metals and casting processes that were beyond his pocket. It was a combination of economic reasons, not a desire to continue Gonzalez' experiments, that gave rise to César's first works (Plates LXIV—LXV).

In this case, too, the sculptor explores the world of horror, peopled by monsters, spurred on by an obsessive desire to step outside the limits of normality, constantly tempted to experiment. César is the interpreter of a present that has not yet acquired a face or a style, that constantly tries to manifest itself without heed to the contradictions that are the price of the vitality (albeit ephemeral) of its expression. Why tie oneself up in any sort of definition? César asked himself; free from any convention or preconception, he considers all experience and experiment possible and acceptable, since they exist. His curiosity has a whole world open before it — and not only the world of the *informe* (shapeless), incomprehensible for a public visually educated by academic naturalism.

With his extreme conceptions, César refuses any contribution from the Purism of avant-garde pioneers, from Constructivism or Neoplasticism. He himself declares,

"I improvise with the material. I touch the material...and hope." And his hope immediately takes form in the works that are closest to Germaine Richier: *Seated Nude* (1954), *Marionettes* (1955), *Scorpion* (1955), and *Bat* (1955—56). His *Nude* is composed of old pieces of scrap iron, and could be considered an object lesson in expressionist anatomy: the body seen from inside, the prototype of the variations on the theme of worn-out mechanisms pioneered by De Chirico's visceral archaeology. The work has nothing in common with the toy motorcar that becomes the muzzle of Picasso's monkey. Each fragment loses its original identity and becomes a tendon, a vein, a muscle, a heart, a lung, in the most absurd of fantastic anatomies. And the ugly *Marionettes*? César peoples a landscape deserted by man, with mantis-like scorpions and giant bats. *Bat* itself is an ingenious construction of wire in the form of a baroque festoon. With the rhythm that gives it life, it might almost be a mobile.

Wall Sculpture (1955) anticipates other, more recent constructions, similar to low reliefs, made of pieces of old automobile coachwork, red and black, shiny and matte. But it is most of all in *Grand Duchess* (1955—56), *Race* (1956), and *Petit Valentin* (1957) that César experiments with assemblage as an idiom of artistic creation, uniting the most disparate fragments in a compact structure — pieces of tubing, wire, scraps of metal — as in the 1958 *Nude* or the diabolical, aggressive, sharply pointed *Insect* (1959). Iron is a flexible material, presenting no obstacles to the sculptor's creative drive, and also the material best suited to his manual skill. César is a smith who sets out to construct his sculpture piece by piece, guided by the infallible, almost magnetic attraction of his sensibility and plastic intelligence, without too precise an idea of the final product.

"All the forms I have in me," says César, "become distorted according to necessity. Everything becomes organized in terms of each part of the work and the thing itself. A work can always turn into something else. One could keep on starting over again indefinitely."

The precarious nature of execution, by comparison with the traditional preparation of work through studies and sketches, is one of the many signs of our times, hostile to the idea of the masterpiece and dedicated to the critical moment of enlightenment or inspired association of ideas, with a charge of vitality concentrated in the crucial instant. The precariousness of life itself is expressed in works that might just as well have taken completely different forms. César's spiritual freedom is directly related to his love of adventure and discovery. *Turtle* (1958), *Homage to Nicolas de Staël* (1958), *Berlingot* (1958), and *Orpheus* (1959) show how the basic structure of sculpture becomes square or rectangular, and how the artist applies the principle of amalgam — that is, the mixture of heterogeneous objects welded together on the same plane according to a more organic constructive method. *Homage to Nicolas de Staël* is conceived as a straightforward three-dimensional transposition of that painter's characteristic surfaces composed of superimposed rectangular expanses of color. For all his exuberant temperament, which leaves him open to all kinds of adventure, César still keeps a rare sense of humor. Factories and auto graveyards are his "studios"; industrial machinery provides his working implements; automatic presses and shears are manipulated with the same sure hand as soldering irons, the same ease as pincers or hammers. César comes alive in the creative gesture, which imparts its vital energy to the plastic murals and "compressions."

54

Figure 11 - André Bloc (1896-): *Flight,* bronze, 1959.

He began with insects and monsters, and has not forgotten them in the course of his feverish activity. Still, his search, usually through different means of expression, tends to give surprising results. Among a regiment of dry branches and twigs (today the mantis corresponds to the Apollo of Classical times) the 1956 *Torso* stands apart, composed of pieces of iron welded and fused together with the oxyhydrogen flame — that is, with a technique designed to replace bronze and casting. It is a full-blown, baroque torso in the tradition of Rodin and Richier, a homage to the pieces dug up in archaeological excavations, with the corrosion and patina of time. The relationship between Richier and César is clearly explained by the affinities of style shown in this singular work.

The possible results of the parallel influences of Giacometti and Richier in the formation of a mannered, decorative style can be seen in the sculpture of Robert Couturier (1905–). Müller and Jacobsen have the same Surrealist sources, but naturally the results are very different.

Robert Müller (1920–) is a terribly serious artisan who works in iron, and shows no sign of humor even when he works with objects discovered in the rusty scrapheaps of the Paris *banlieue.* His early sculptures give the effect of genuine harrows or plows. A sado-sexual obsession dominates his later work, swollen out with metal elements brutally welded together, punctuated with scythe- or lance-points, like stolid, grave

55

heraldic figures (Plates LXVI–LXVII). Müller's Surrealist world is as dark as the smoke from a factory chimney, tangled and confused, and expresses in forms drawn from medieval German armor and fossilized crustacea a bizarre mixture of culture and nature: a world at once zoomorphic and phytomorphic, with violent, excessive, Nordically inspired effects and constant allusions to the violence and cruelty of our own times.

Robert Jacobsen (1912–), who has lived in Paris since 1947, shows the same craftsmanly qualities that distinguish Müller. He works with cold iron, bending it with hammers to avoid weakening the metal with fire. After a period of Constructivist pseudo-rigor with overtones of Gonzalez and allusions to Surrealist objects, Jacobsen devoted himself to the manufacture (in the most exact etymological sense of the word) of fetish-figurines recalling rediscovered models of avant-garde art, from North America to Oceania, South America to Asia. Jacobsen's sense of the fantastic has become more and more bizarre, creating a host of statuettes that must be placed in the category of eccentric art, strictly cultural in origin (Plate LXVIII).

In a world of iron "technicians," Müller and Jacobsen stand apart as two smiths who use the methods of the past, with a rigorous sense of métier corresponding exactly to the limits of their surreal imagination.

In *Tightrope Walkers* and *The Last of the Acrobats* (Plate LXIX), Costas Coulentianos (1918–), who works in iron and bronze, places his sculptures in an upward-soaring position, as if in a sort of irregular trajectory in space. Other works, however, are composted of massive volumes linked together with iron disks and bands, which enclose them in a sort of cage — a symbol of the times?

Nicolas Schöffer (1912–) constructs other cages, composed of metal trellises, assembled along strictly Constructivist lines, which seem veritable mechanized labyrinths. Schöffer is the father of all mobile sculpture, or rather, automobile sculpture, in which a little motor hidden in the bowels of the work sets off rhythmic movements, very different, naturally, from the movements of Alexander Calder's "leaves," which flutter through space at the touch of a hand or the slightest breeze.

Lattices, perforated surfaces, complicated mechanical elements reconstructed in spatiodynamic reality, that is, in a synthesis of spatial and dynamic constructive elements, constitute the framework in which the sculptor can "use space as the basic material." To quote Schöffer, "Spatiodynamic sculpture is not hermetic; it is a spectacle in counterpoint with man and the environment."

With the addition of the motor and natural or artificial light, the spatiodynamic complex can reproduce highly intense visual combinations in color or black and white on virtually any surface. Furthermore, Schöffer supplements this complicated mechanism with recorded sounds, "percussive elements treated electronically" with a view to creating a synthesis of painting, sculpture, music, and cinema. The demand for an integration of the arts makes itself strongly felt in the work and thought of this sculptor.

In *Lux 4* of 1957 (Plate LXXI) the play of light is composed and decomposed by the continual metamorphosis of the structure, through which this work of advanced engineering becomes something else: a sculpture, in a synthesis of the various contributions of the other arts. Often the results express the spirit of a typically mechanized industrial society, with overtones of playfulness and scientific parody. Schöffer has executed some extremely tall sculptures — between one and two hundred feet high — which, like skyscrapers, are true symbols of their times. But his constant aim is to link his spatiodynamic investigations to the dynamics of light. He is an inventor who makes science-poetry as others write science fiction. The experiments of Gabo and a long tradition of avant garde are resumed in Schöffer's work, which is based on the desire to represent our time through the symbols of technical and scientific progress, using the real movement of light and mechanisms, which give art a new, unprecedented dimension.

Besides the Richier-César stream and the Constructivist, technological imagination of Schöffer, modern French sculpture contains another current of research, this time close to the original life of the elements. Here, vegetable and mineral structures inspire a new organic language, rich in suggestion and with great possibilities for development — represented by Stahly, Étienne Martin, and Alicia Penalba.

François Stahly (1911—) became friends with Étienne Martin when he began work in the Académie Ranson in 1931. His solidarity with the sculptor from Loriol seems almost inevitable in view of their identical cultural interests, their common study of pagan and Christian secret rites. Discovery of nature in an epoch very prone to confuse art and science, because of the miracles of technological progress (applied illusionistically to the arts), is for Stahly the fruit of methodical research conducted in the spirit of a Klee.

Wood is the most suitable material for experimenting with the organic growth of forms, in *Star I* (1959–60), *Large Bird* (1960), *Birth* of 1955 (Plate LXXIII), *Park Sculpture* (1959–61), and *The Guardian* of 1961 (Plate LXXII), which are close to the formal world of Étienne Martin. These are organic forms that develop like branches in the space of a more solid trunk: roots and branches wrenched from the earth, and other plants like swollen bulbs; formless sculptures, as Stahly describes them, "because they cannot be subjected to geometrical analysis."

Indeed, this type of analysis would be impossible, insofar as Stahly's sculptures are natural entanglements generated by the earth, following the movement of growth in different directions. This impression becomes stronger when one notices how naturally Stahly's wood sculptures stand on their flat surfaces, as if they had hidden roots and ties. There are no formulas or *a priori* solutions in the art of Stahly, who once said to Carola Giedion-Welcker, "Groping unconsciously toward possible meaning, that's our myth." And the one possible myth is the myth of a search, which so often seems obscure, aimed at discovering the significance and inner reason of these forms beyond their external appearance.

The bronze reliefs of *The Creation of the World* (1960), the wooden *Chains* made in 1960 and exhibited the following year, and the large metal constructions studied and elaborated in Meudon, where Stahly has gathered round himself a circle of pupils and collaborators just as in a Renaissance workshop, complete our idea of the sculptor's personality. The tendency toward collective collaboration is another sign of the times, which no longer have any place for the cult of the individual or the masterpiece myth. The humility of common research, sustained by faith in an ideal, whether religious, social, or human, is a highly educational, essentially moral result of the master's work.

For far too long, discussion of art has been limited to a narrow circle of specialists, or a clearly defined sector of society. Stahly, turning back to a study of natural elements, found in himself a driving impulse, alien to intellectualist doctrine, to increase the humanity and truth in his sculpture, which is pervaded by an inner rhythm of ardent spirituality.

The same problem faces the sculpture of Étienne Martin (1913–), in the context of a most mysterious and slightly ambiguous surreality. Martin is indeed the sculptor of the surreal; at times he even showed leanings toward the Surrealists themselves. His meeting with Marcel Duchamp in 1935 was of great value to him at a critical moment in his artistic formation. Duchamp was the master of unconfined liberty, the nonconformist, the inventor of new forms. Étienne Martin's destiny was to take shape from 1947 on, closely linked to Stahly's, precisely in terms of affinities of choice. In his *Couples and Dragons* (1955–57), Étienne Martin's sculpture is more solid, more compact, hacked out of the great trunks with an imperious, baroque breadth. Branches, roots, trunks, transformed by art, appear in a new reality as primordial organic forms. Stahly and Martin have imposed a type of "vegetable vision" based on the most contorted, dramatic associations and allusions, which identifies with the most fantastic accidental sculptures provided by uprooted or half-cut trees in the forest. The two sculptors have helped us to see beyond appearances into the symbolic morphology of nature (not for the sake of ironic humor, as is the case of Dubuffet, nor because of a penchant for the grotesque). Étienne Martin is a collector of bizarre objects, revealed first by Surrealism, as documental evidence of hidden truths. With modern man's passion for fetishes, he projects his fantastic humor in these objects, showing in his incredible choices every fact or element of reality in the most rare and unexpected forms. In these cases, sculpture becomes a means of visual investigation, which then becomes a poetic inquiry into the most mysterious aspects of nature. It is said that Étienne Martin admires Bernini: a new confirmation of the link between surreality and the baroque.

Recently, the sculptor has set out, in the series of *Demeures* (*Dwellings*) spanning the period 1956–60 and initiated with *Homage to Lovercraft*, to build complicated, labyrinthine sculptures in the unity of a new formal conception. They are similar to the tomb-cells and columbaria of a cemetery, inspired by the theme of night. In his *Demeures*, Étienne Martin interprets even the humblest bricks inserted in baroque-inspired "interiors" which, rather than allude to the most secret germinations of life, reproduce the space in which man lives and disappears, in a fantastic transposition that is both lugubrious and enigmatic. As Carola Giedion-Welcker says, Étienne Martin and Stahly "have led our times and our artistic sensibility back to the primordial life of the elements." Here we have a new reaction, wider and deeper, against the rationalist cult of form and all the derivations of Constructivism, Purism, or Neoplasticism that proposed the concept of the work of art governed by the Golden Number, by divine proportion or the technical data of advanced science.

Alicia Penalba (1918–) builds her fantastic world out of memories and suggestions of a far-off land that has remained in her imagination to become the source of inexhaustible inspiration. Arriving in Paris from Buenos Aires, Penalba entered Zadkine's studio in 1948 and began to show, in the 1952 Salon de la Jeune Sculpture, her characteristic vegetable totems, adopted as abstract modules for variations on the theme of cacti and tropical trees and flowers. Her compositions are vertical, with occasional hints at Cubism in the structural plan and certain points of contact with Stahly and Étienne Martin. New developments appeared in 1958, especially in *Sea Creatures* that recall flowers opening out in fleshy petals. Her totems, like the "columns" and "chains" are monuments to natural forces. And the germination of forms in *Counterpoint* (1959) and *Multiple Lovers* (1960), not to mention *Project for a Fountain* (1959), always leads back to a relationship with earth and origins, with greater liberty in movement and rhythm expressed simultaneously in several directions.

Alicia Penalba has found her natural environment in the most feverish artistic circles of Paris, and the naturalness of her sculptures, from *Cathedral* of 1958 (Plate LXXVI) to *Sculpture Project for a Children's Playground* of 1961 (Plate LXXVII), which strain upward or articulate horizontally, seems to spring from the secret reality of things. And this is the inner reality that the most sensitive of modern artists consider with continually renewed curiosity and a desire to reduce it to the imaginary substance of their surreal works. *Apocalyptic Childhood* (1959) has the same evocative power as Étienne Martin's *Demeures*.

Stanislas Wostan (1915—) made his mark on the informal expressionist milieu with a few works, such as the *Grand Duke* of 1952 (Plate LXXIX), the 1958 bronze *Sculpture*, and the beaten-copper relief *Twilight* of 1959 (Plate LXXVIII), rather than with the other works he has shown in the main Parisian group exhibits. Wostan, who came to Paris from Poland after suffering the tribulations of war and persecution, is still tied to the memories of his tragic past and has exteriorized them in sculpture, unleashing an immense expressive charge. His almost savage urge to express himself has led him to search constantly for new materials, exhausting them in the course of thorough experiments. *Grand Duke* is made of terra cotta and crushed brick set in cement and painted. Wostan also works in colored plaster, uses prefabricated constructional elements, shows an assured technique in his handling of metals — bronze, copper, brass, sheet iron — and impregnates every work with a romantic, passionate content inspired by the tragic reality of the world he has so unhappily lived in.

This content is to be found in much of today's sculpture, a profoundly human content that becomes almost a social experience by virtue of events suffered in common.

As we have already seen several times, all the younger sculptors, including Wostan, tend toward surreal expression, which may be the current means of expressing subjective feelings rather than external facts. The trend toward universality of content is another sign of the collective process that is linking together the arts of all countries. Humanity has suffered too much, and humanity still suffers too much for contemporary art not to have come to interpret the profoundest sense of human suffering, approaching it with the conscious will power of a Klee, approaching the mystery that divides and strikes down human spirits.

The recurring images of the continual call of nature become even more acute and tense in the aerodynamic *Birds* of Charles Delahaye (1928—), in the movement of formless fragments hurled into space and pinned down at a point in their trajectory. The *Birds* develops into *Horsemen* and later into *Aviatiques*. Delahaye, with his extremely personal point of view, always chose the surreal world for his first inspirations which later, in the 1958 *Figures*, took on a more decisive plastic consistency and accentuated dynamic rhythm. His sculptural conceptions are better defined in the 1961 *Samurai* (Plate LXXXI) and *Standard* (Plate LXXX) in a turbulent, disquieting synthesis of organic forms dominated by an inner energy that pervades the whole, like blood coursing through veins. The call he makes on the obscure forces of nature is also evident in his female figures.

One of the youngest sculptors in France, Delahaye is also an artist who has most clearly formulated his own aims and individuality, often overcoming the difficulties opposing such a formulation that are presented by the specious aesthetic doctrines or clan solidarity which surround and support modish movements.

With Delahaye we conclude this panorama of French modern sculpture. However, we must at least mention the names of Louis Chavignier (1922–) and Jean-Pierre Duprey, whose initial Surrealism was influenced first by Art Nouveau then by Stahly, and Michel Guino (1928–) and Philippe Hiquily (1925–). Guino constructs airy, cellular objects in iron, held in daring equilibrium, while Hiquily invents surprising Surrealist works that betray his reverence for Marcel Duchamp and the early Giacometti.

Each and every one of these has made and is making his own contribution in investigation, experiment, and essay, using traditional materials and methods or exploiting new media and techniques borrowed from industry; out of this collective effort, the product of so many fiercely individual personalities, emerge the main lines of contemporary sculpture, inspired by a newly discovered relationship with nature and its most jealously hidden forces.

The modern artist is not a mere entertainer, nor is he engulfed in the polemical activity of the first avant-garde movements of the century. The sculptor today aims at using every possible means to penetrate, with the greatest possible freedom of inquiry, into the world in which we seem to exist, the space we move through, creating statues and monuments and objects that represent a desperate longing to know or an anxious denunciation of the fear, distrust, and uncertainty that oppress the spirit of contemporary man.

It is not easy to make a synthesis of the history of modern French sculpture in its development from Rodin's *Balzac* to the present day. The most prominent personalities reveal and affirm themselves in isolation, often above the great movements and currents of taste determined by the poetics and aesthetics formulated by philosophers and artists. From Bergson's philosophy of intuition to Sartre's existentialism, from the words of Rodin and Apollinaire's writings to the notebooks of Laurens and Stahly, we can follow the wave of ideas and inquiry for a whole century. The problems of sculpture break away from traditional, three-dimensional Classicism, static and frozen in the canons of formal beauty and academic techniques, and move toward the concept of open, multi-dimensional sculpture, executed with the newest materials and methods, often definitively rejecting figuration.

With his representations of *Balzac*, Rodin had already sensed a type of plastic truth that did not harmonize with the naturalism of the nineteenth century. All early twentieth-century artists, from Matisse to Duchamp-Villon, looked on him as a sculptor guided by infallible instinct to the most audacious solutions. Rodin wanted to be another Michelangelo, in the heyday of Art Nouveau, and his titanic side found its outlet in the *Gates of Hell*, which are a sort of Divine Comedy interpreted in flamboyant style, but with the figures of the damned hurtling into space with an impetus so great that it was to influence the inner dynamics and moving forms of later sculp-

Figure 12 - César Baldaccini (1921-): *The House of Davotte*, 1960.

tures. Beside this type of experiment, in which Duchamp-Villon excelled, we have the affirmation of the painterly Cubism of Picasso and Braque, Gris and Laurens, translated into the three-dimensional, mixed-media constructions of Laurens, Lipchitz, Archipenko, Zadkine, and Csaky, which were later to degenerate into conventionalized, mannered formulas. Showing greater cultural independence, Picasso, after experimenting with Cubist compositions based on wood and colored cardboard, which had an immense success and were continued by Schwitters and Ernst, passed on to the most incredible neoclassical and Surrealist experiments.

Sculpture by painters, with the nineteenth-century examples of Daumier, Degas, and Gauguin, continued in the twentieth century with the elegant Expressionist figures of Matisse, the elemental primitivism of Derain, the stylism of Braque, and the ironic or eccentric essays of Dubuffet or Fautrier. Picasso cannot be placed in this category, as he might just as well be considered a sculptor who paints. His output spans half a century, from the *Harlequin* reminiscent of Rodin and Rosso to the cutout metal *Bathers*; passing through an endless variety of expression, from African fetishes to the naturalism of *Goat*; from the Gonzalez-inspired irons to the inventive Surrealist still-life objects. Gonzalez, the absolute pioneer not only of the application of autogenic welding to sculpture, but also of the use of iron as an expressive material, inaugurates the modern iron age. Beside the broad lines of development represented by these exceptional personalities, Brancusi appears as an independent, tending toward the absolute purity of the image and its formal perfection, with a view to the work's durability. Arp, after the Dada experiment, creates a sculptural idiom of autonomous, organic forms, abstractly conceived yet at the same time always rich in reality and generally born of a sensual intuition. Giacometti makes his appearance in the context of Surrealist intellectualism, creating memorable objects, but becomes increasingly dissatisfied with himself and moves from crisis to crisis, finally proposing a new figuration based on a point of view that goes from the particular to the general, from the close to the infinitely far. Giacometti's elongated figures belong to a culture based on archaeology and primitive arts considered as examples of expressive purity.

In the Surrealist field, with a curiosity that often leads itself to contradiction, Max Ernst gives life to his own cultural phantoms.

Brancusi is the prototype of the principle of ideal purity in modern sculpture; Pevsner is the fanatical theorist of Constructivism applied to the plastic arts, using transparent, flexible, modern materials, then bronze elements and networks of brass spun out in space like theorems. One of the survivors of the De Stijl group, Vantongerloo is a Constructivist who aimed at creating sculpture out of architectonic elements.

The various movements and personalities of our century did not and do not exist in isolation in hermetically sealed compartments. There have always been very active interchanges between even the most incompatible theoretical positions. It is thus difficult to establish just how much is due to one or the other in the various sectors of modern sculpture. One could talk of the spirit of collective research, to which everyone contributed according to his means; but one must also mention the polemical contrasts and controversial skirmishes. The masters we have spoken of have been succeeded by entire generations of artists who carry on, in different directions, the inquiries already undertaken, or open up new ones. Gilioli, Hajdu, and Lipsi move along the lines laid down by Purism, each one working on his own problems, as did Chauvin.

62

Another, very different path leads Béothy, Stahly, Étienne Martin, and Alicia Penalba toward a surreality that has nothing to do with Surrealism, but stems from a new conception of nature and its hidden forces.

Adam proposes with rigorous coherency the problem of integrating the arts (sculpture and architecture in his case) on a monumental scale — this moves toward meeting a need that has made itself felt in the last few years.

An equally important function was fulfilled by Germaine Richier, who can be looked on as the inspiration and guiding force of a whole generation of modern sculptors. Richier gave her own pessimistic interpretation of the forces of nature, hostile to man and seething with monsters; she represented these forces as symbols of obsession and fear — as the cruel apparitions that have become so familiar in contemporary sculpture.

Germaine Richier's surreal vision sparked the ingenious and multiformed fantasies of César, the calmer informal idiom of Delahaye, and the investigations into the character of matter that condition artistic expression in an often chaotic movement of scientific and esoteric curiosity.

All the ideas and all the events of the century are in the sculpture that runs from Rodin to César in a hallucinating race or challenge to the future, modifying the very conception of the nature of sculpture in a continual symbiosis with the other visual arts, so that, after half a century of progressively more daring experiments, we see Maillol's *Action Enchained* turn into an old automobile gliding into a press worked by the diabolical hand of César.

CONCISE BIBLIOGRAPHY

BRIZIO, A. M. - *Ottocento e Novecento*, Turin, 1939

CLARIS, E. - *De l'Impressionnisme en Sculpture*, Paris, 1902

ERNST, M. - *Beyond Painting*, New York, 1948

GIEDION-WELCKER, C. - *Contemporary Sculpture. An Evolution in Volume and Space*, New York, 1955

GISCHIA, L., and VÉDRES, N. - *La Sculpture en France depuis Rodin*, Paris, 1945

GUGGENHEIM, P. - *Art of this Century*, New York, 1942

HOFMANN, W. - *Plastik des 20. Jahrhunderts*, Frankfurt, 1958

JAGUER, E. - *Sculpture 1950-1960. Poétique de la sculpture*, Paris, 1960

JEAN, M. - *Le Surréalisme*, Paris, 1958

MALRAUX, A. - *Le Musée imaginaire de la sculpture mondiale*, Paris, 1960

RITCHIE, A. C. - *Sculpture of the Twentieth Century*, New York, 1953

SEUPHOR, M. - *La Sculpture de ce siècle*, Neuchâtel, 1959 (*The Sculpture of this Century*, New York-London, 1960)

Témoignages pour la sculpture abstraite, Paris, 1956

TRIER, E. - *Moderne Plastik von Rodin bis Marini*, Berlin, 1954

VALENTINER, W. R. - *Origins of Modern Sculpture*, New York, 1946

PLATES

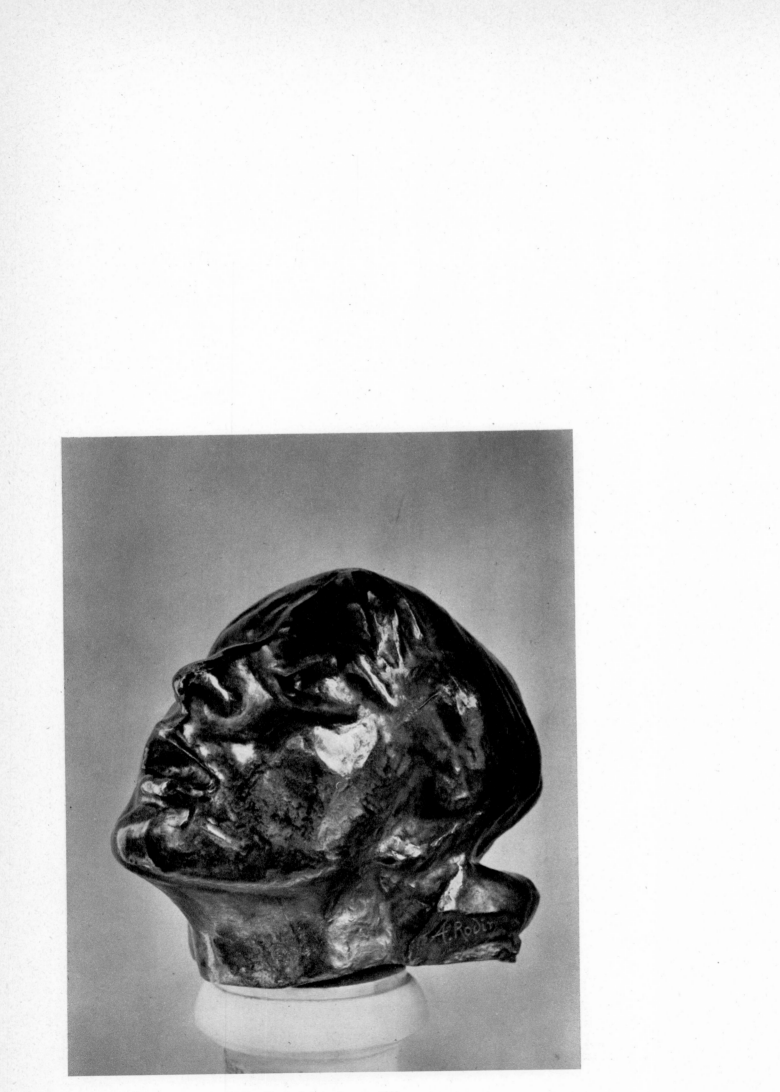

Plate I - Auguste Rodin (1840-1917): *Head of Pain*, bronze, 1892

Plate II - Auguste Rodin: *Monument to Balzac*, bronze, 1893-98

Plate III - Antoine Bourdelle (1861-1929): *Head of Daumier,* plaster, 1929

Plate IV - Antoine Bourdelle: *Penelope*, bronze, 1908

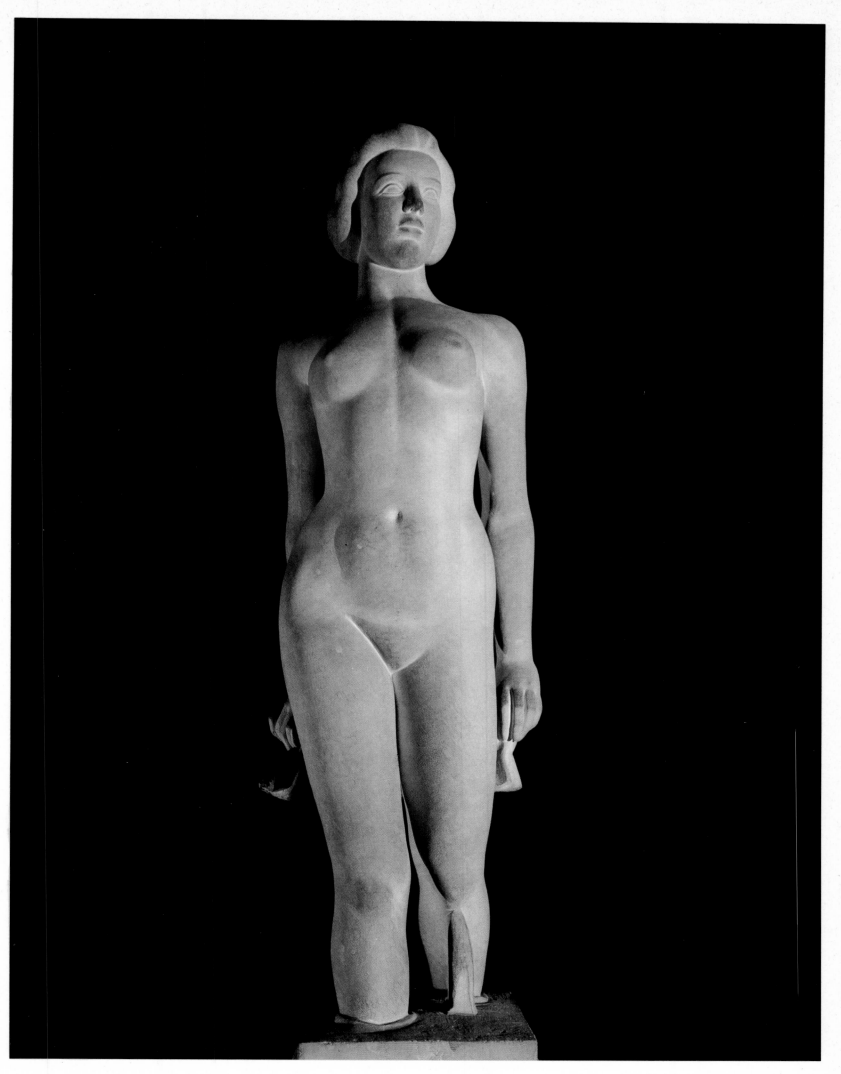

Plate V - Aristide Maillol (1861-1944): *Ile de France*, stone, 1921-25

Plate VI - Aristide Maillol: *The River,* lead, 1939-42

Plate VII - Aristide Maillol: *The River* (detail)

Plate VIII - Charles Despiau (1874-1946): *Eve*, bronze, 1925

Plate IX - Charles Despiau: *Paulette*, plaster, 1907

Plate X - Henri Matisse (1869-1954): *Reclining Nude*, bronze, 1907

Plate XI - Henri Matisse: *Reclining Nude* (detail)

Plate XII - Georges Braque (1882-1963): *The Nile*, bronze, 1942

Plate XIII - Georges Braque: *Horse's Head,* bronze, 1943

Plate XIV - Jean Dubuffet (1901-): *Blind Man,* sheet tin, 1959

Plate XV - Raoul Ubac (1910-): *Torso*, slate, 1960

Plate XVI - Constantin Brancusi (1876-1957): *The Kiss*, stone, 1908

Plate XVII - Constantin Brancusi: *Maiastra*, bronze, 1912

Plate XVIII - Constantin Brancusi: *Bird in Space,* bronze, 1940

Plate XIX - Constantin Brancusi: *Seal*, gray marble, 1943

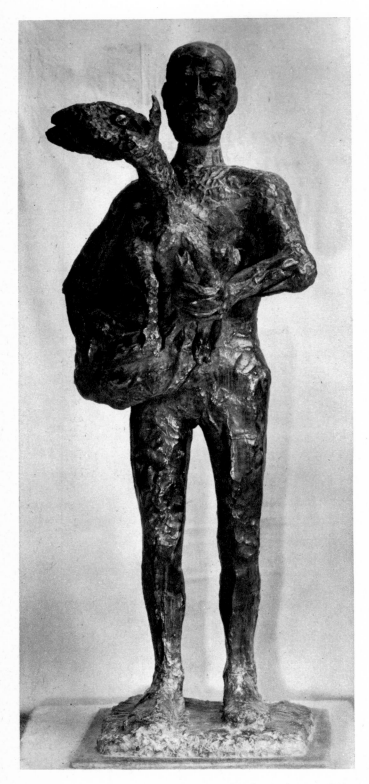

Plate XX - Pablo Picasso (1881-): *Man with Lamb*, bronze, 1944

Plate XXI - Pablo Picasso: *Woman's Head* (Monument to Guillaume Apollinaire), bronze, 1941-44

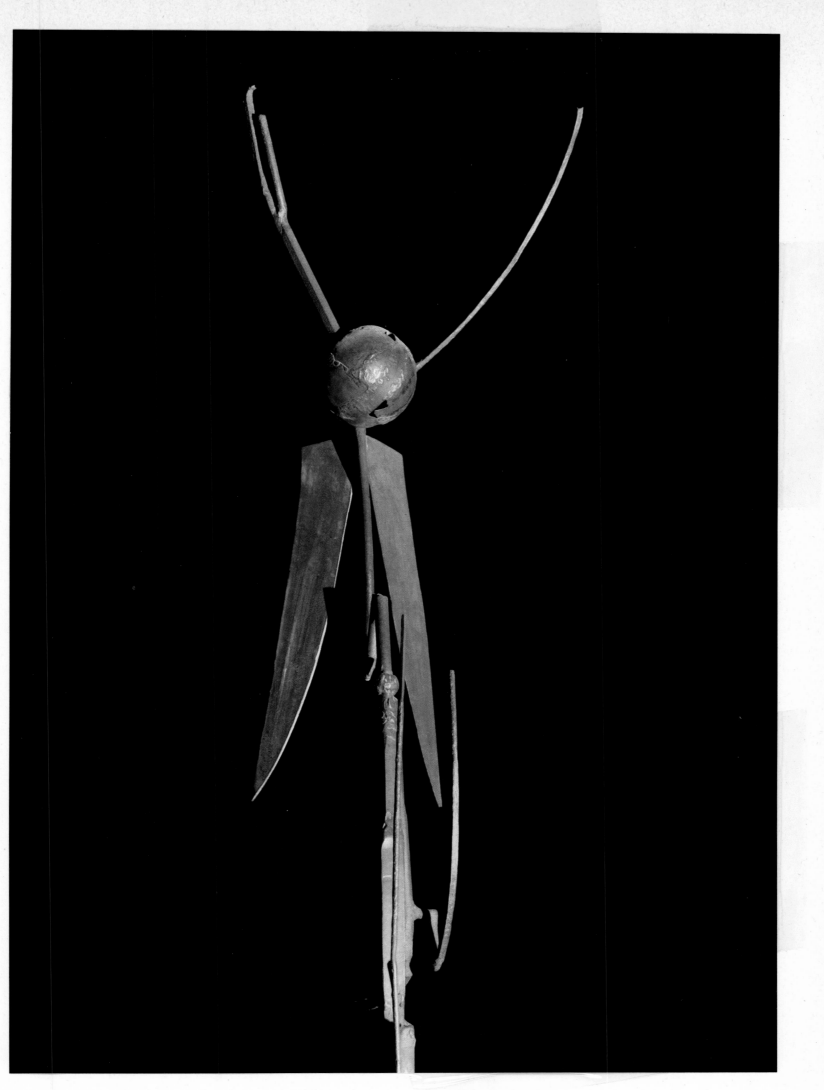

Plate XXII - Julio Gonzalez (1876-1942): *Angel*, iron, 1933

Plate XXIII - Julio Gonzalez: *Head of Montserrat,* bronze, 1942

Plate XXIV - Pablo Gargallo (1881-1934): *Harlequin with Flute*, bronze, 1933

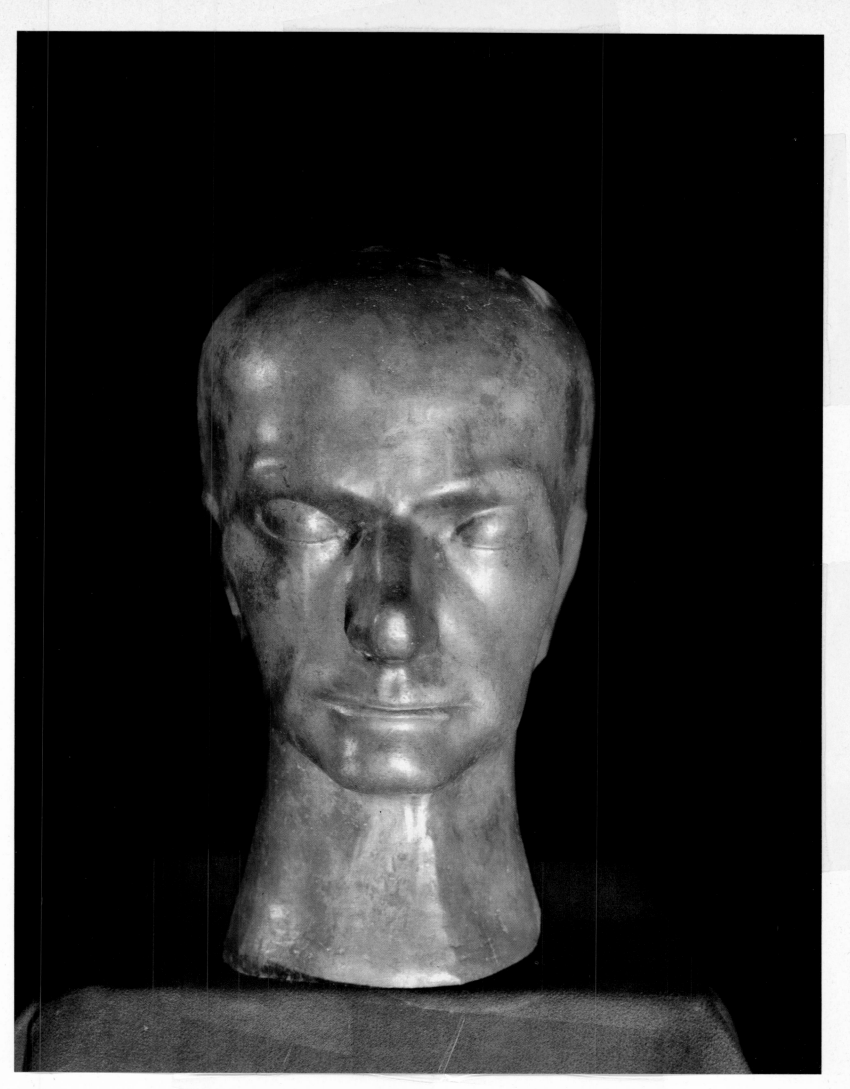

Plate XXV - Raymond Duchamp-Villon (1876-1918): *Baudelaire*, bronze, 1911

Plate XXVI - Raymond Duchamp-Villon: *Horse's Head,* bronze, 1914

Plate XXVII - Henri Laurens (1885-1956): *Man with Pipe*, stone, 1919

Plate XXVIII - Henri Laurens: *The Farewell*, bronze, 1941

Plate XXIX - Henri Laurens: *Seated Woman*, bronze, 1932

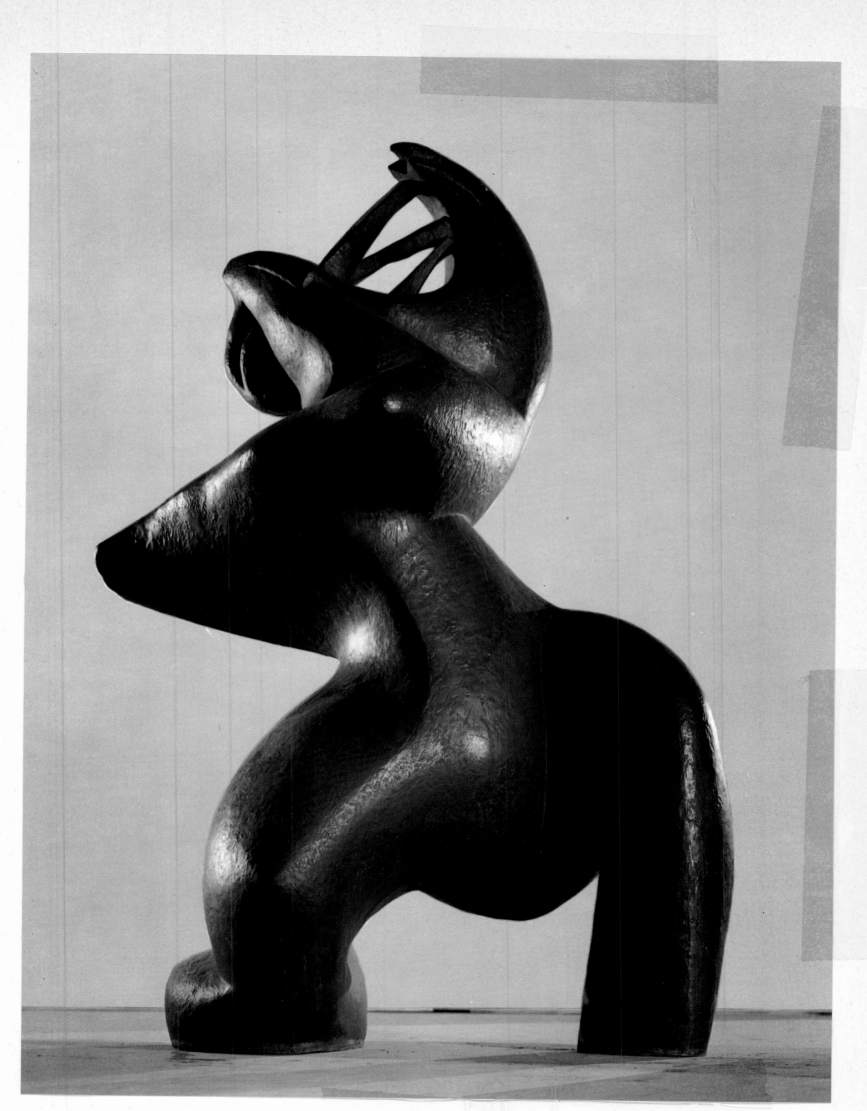

Plate XXX - Henri Laurens: *Large Musician*, bronze, 1950

Plate XXXI - Jacques Lipchitz (1891-): *Sailor with Guitar*, gilt-bronze, 1914

Plate XXXII - Jacques Lipchitz: *Figure*, bronze, 1926-30

Plate XXXIII - Jacques Lipchitz: *Song of the Vowels*, bronze, 1930-32

Plate XXXIV - Jacques Lipchitz: *The Rape of Europa*, bronze, 1938

Plate XXXV - Ossip Zadkine (1890-): *Female Figures*, lava, 1918

Plate XXXVI - Ossip Zadkine: *The Maenads*, bronze, 1932

Plate XXXVII - Joseph Csaky (1888-): *Relief*, stone, 1920

Plate XXXVIII - Joseph Csaky: *Standing Woman*, gilt-bronze, 1913

Plate XXXIX - Louis Chauvin (1889-): *Couple*, wood, 1940

Plate XL - Louis Chauvin: *Don Juan*, bronze, 1945

Plate XLI - Étienne Béothy (1897–1961): *Interlocking Rhythms*. wood, 1937

Plate XLII - Jean (Hans) Arp (1887-): *Construction of White Flowers in Memory of a Dead Woman,*
painted wood, 1943

Plate XLIII - Jean (Hans) Arp: *Wreath of Breasts,* marble, 1945

Plate XLIV - Jean (Hans) Arp: *Shepherd of the Clouds*, bronze, 1953

Plate XLV - Jean (Hans) Arp: *Idol,* bronze, 1950

Plate XLVI - Antoine Pevsner (1884-1962): *Dynamic Construction*, bronze, 1957

Plate XLVII - Antoine Pevsner: *Extensible Surface Construction*, plaster and bronze, 1941

Plate XLVIII - Antoine Pevsner: *Embryonic Construction*, bronze, 1948

Plate XLIX - Antoine Pevsner: *Extensible Surface,* silvered bronze, 1941

Plate L - Alberto Giacometti (1901-): *The Piazza*, bronze, 1948-49

Plate LI - Alberto Giacometti: *Diego,* bronze, 1960

Plate LII - Max Ernst (1891-): *King Playing with Queen*, bronze, 1954

Plate LIII - Max Ernst: *Bird-Head*, bronze, 1956

Plate LIV - Henri-Georges Adam (1904-): *Monumental Sculpture for the Le Havre Museum*, cement, 1959

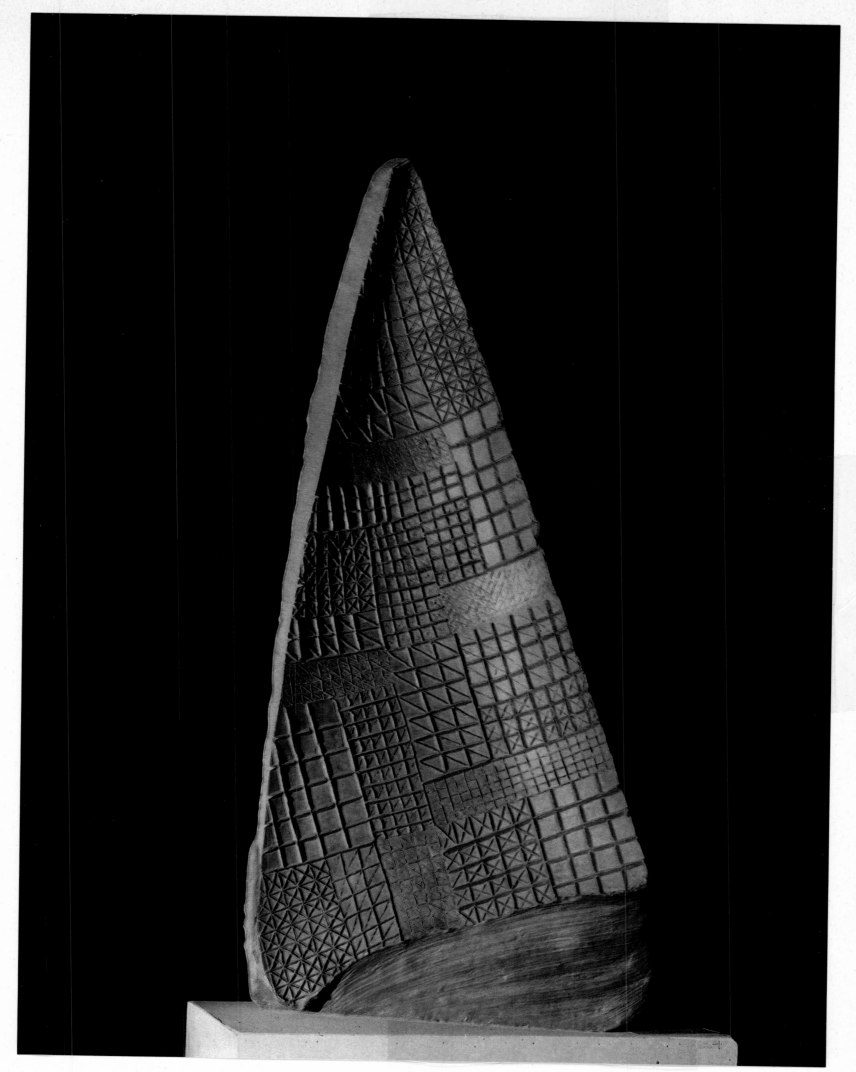

Plate LV - Henri-Georges Adam: *The Wave*, gilt-bronze, 1959

Plate LVI - Emile Gilioli (1911-): *Saint Martin*, Alpine granite, 1958

Plate LVII - Emile Gilioli: *Isolina,* marble, 1949-56

Plate LVIII - Morice Lipsi (1898-): *Lava Sculpture*, lava, 1961

Plate LIX - Morice Lipsi: *Structure*, lava, 1961

Plate LX - Étienne Hajdu (1907-): *The Girls of My Town*, marble, 1961

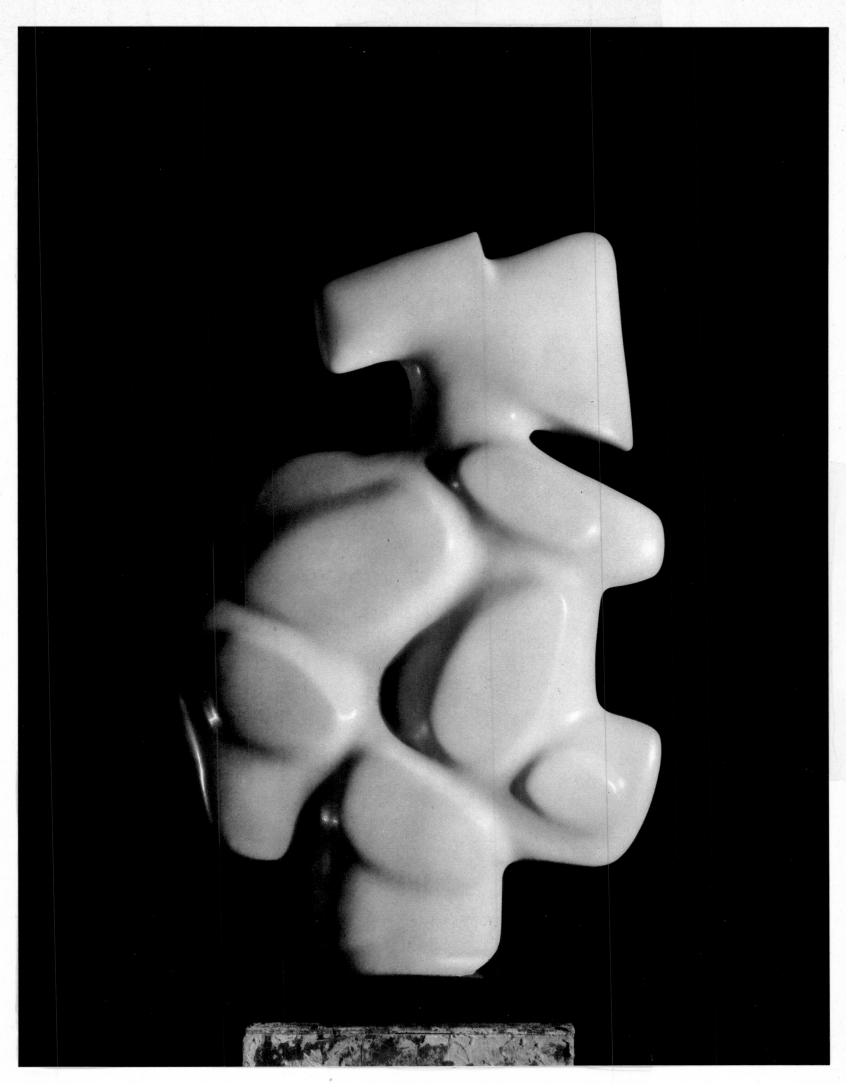

Plate LXI - Étienne Hajdu: *Sculpture A.*, marble, 1961

Plate LXII - Germaine Richier (1904-1959): *Storm*, bronze, 1947-48

Plate LXIII - Germaine Richier: *Storm* (detail)

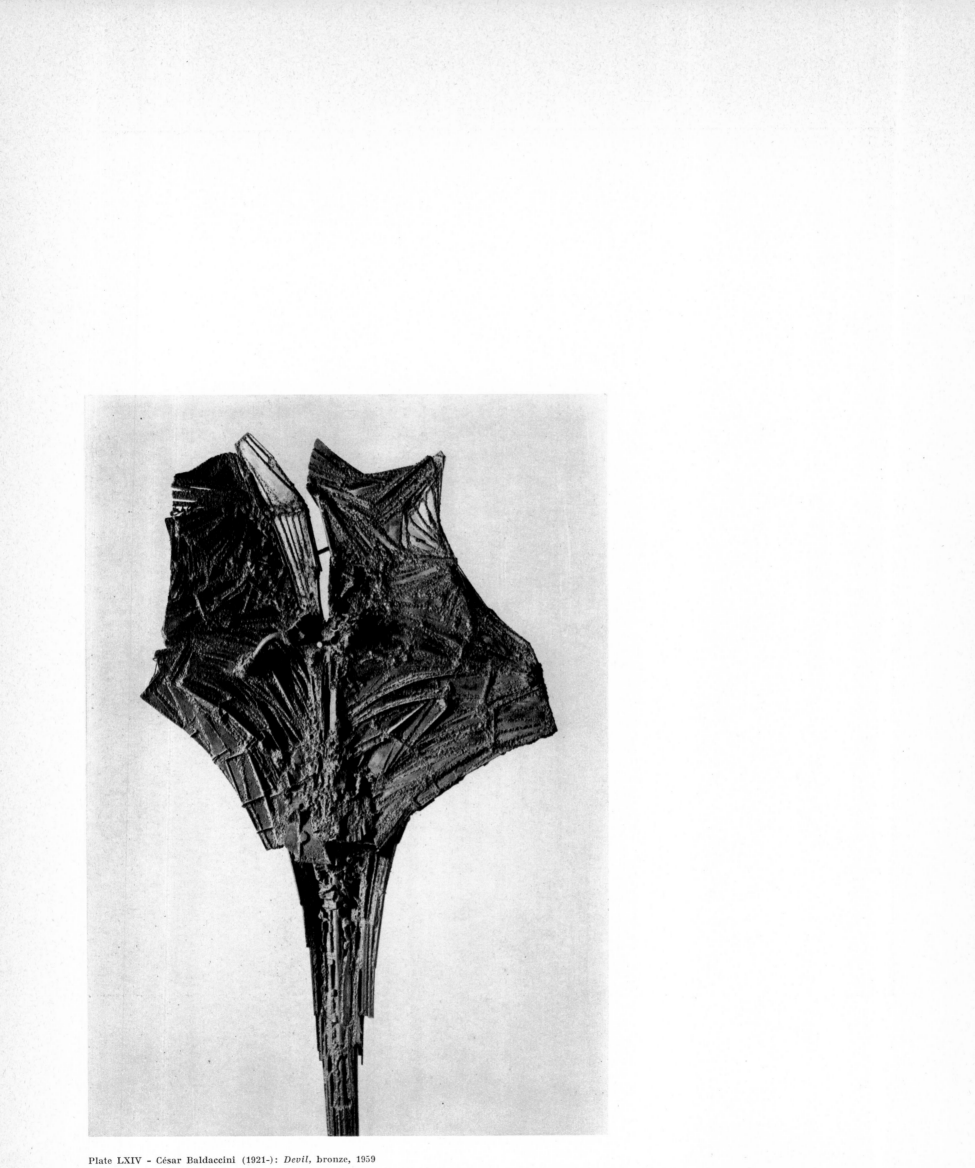

Plate LXIV - César Baldaccini (1921-): *Devil*, bronze, 1959

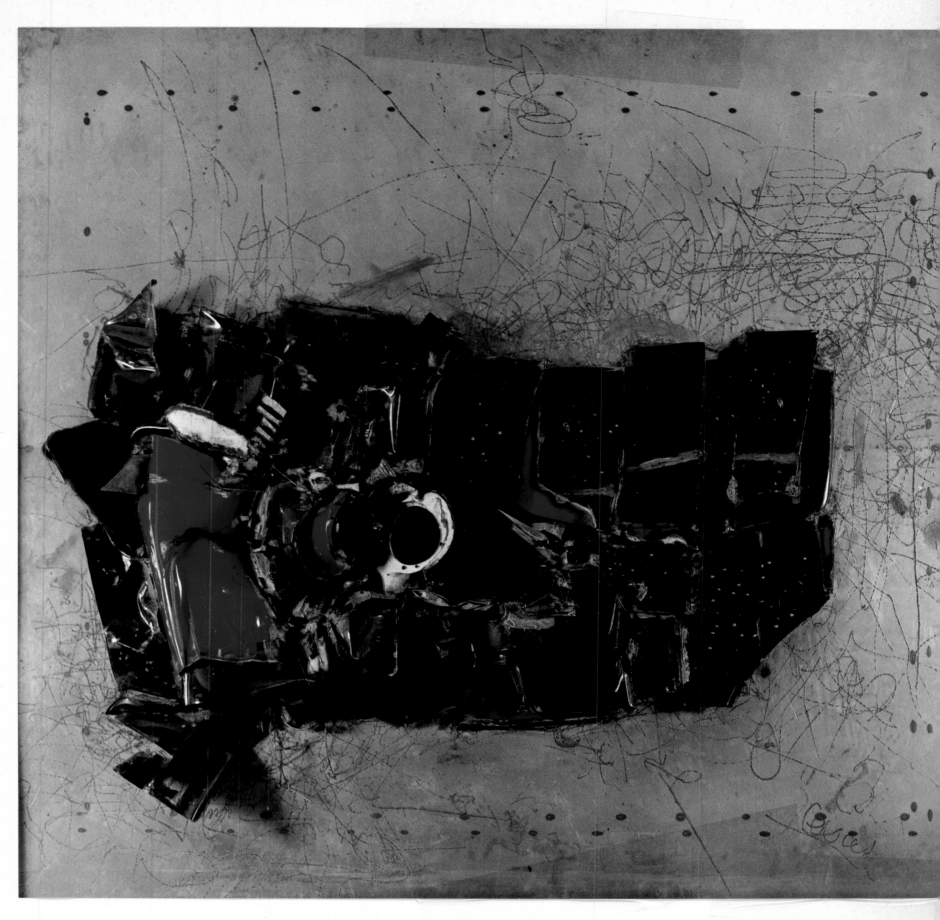

Plate LXV – César Baldaccini: *Composition,* iron and colored sheet metal, 1960

Plate LXVI - Robert Müller (1920-): *Relief*, iron, 1957

Plate LXVII - Robert Müller: *Usurper*, iron, 1959

Plate LXVIII - Robert Jacobsen (1912-): *Hengesit,* iron, 1958

Plate LXIX - Costas Coulentianos (1918-): *The Last of the Acrobats*, iron and lead, 1960

Plate LXX - Nicolas Schöffer (1912-): *Spatiodynamic Sculpture*, iron, 1954

Plate LXXI - Nicolas Schöffer: *Lux 4* (Luminodynamic complex), 1957

Plate LXXII - François Stahly (1911-): *The Guardian*, wood, 1961

Plate LXXIII - François Stahly: *Birth,* wood, 1955

Plate LXXIV - Étienne Martin (1913-): *Dragon,* wood, 1956

Plate LXXV - Étienne Martin: *Large Dragon*, wood, 1947

Plate LXXVI - Alicia Penalba (1918-): *Cathedral*, bronze, 1958

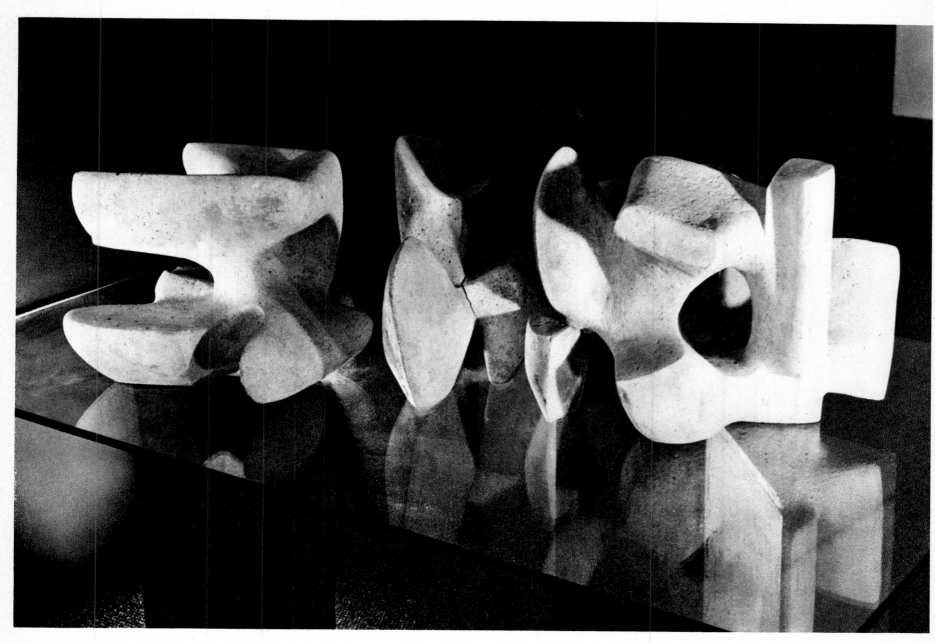

Plate LXXVII - Alicia Penalba: *Sculpture Project for a Children's Playground*, stone, 1961

Plate LXXVIII - Stanislas Wostan (1915-): *Twilight*, beaten copper, 1959

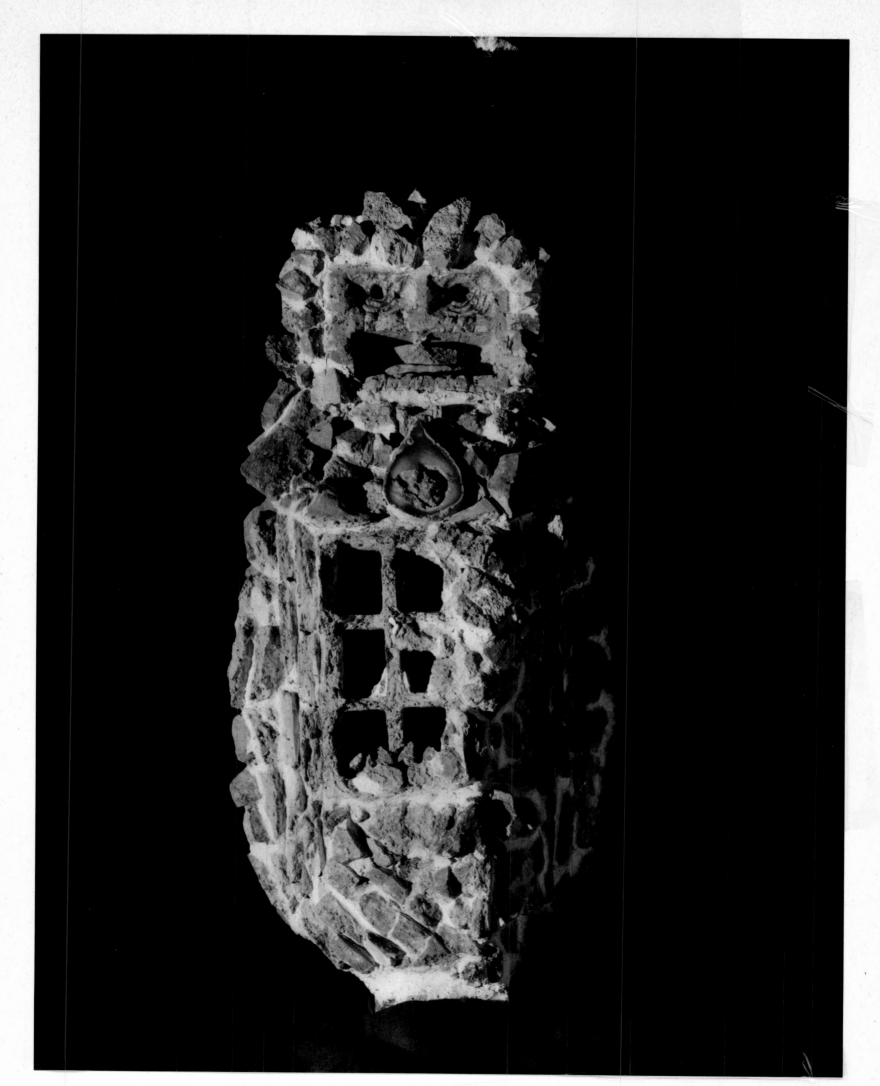

Plate LXXIX - Stanislas Wostan: *Grand-Duke*, crushed brick and colored cement, 1952

Plate LXXX - Charles Delahaye (1928-): *Standard* (second version), bronze, 1961

Plate LXXXI - Charles Delahaye: *Samurai* (second version), bronze, 1961

LIST OF ILLUSTRATIONS

Note: The illustrations in the text have Arabic numerals; all others Roman numerals. An asterisk (*) preceding the number indicates a colorplate.